D0522841

EUROPE: IN OR OUT?

EUROPE: IN OR OUT?
Everything You Need to Know

DAVID CHARTER

Biteback Publishing

First published in Great Britain in 2014 by
Biteback Publishing Ltd
Westminster Tower
3 Albert Embankment
London SE1 7SP
Copyright © David Charter 2014

ISBN 978-184954-684-3

10 9 8 7 6 5 4 3 2 1

A CIP catalogue record for this book is available from the British Library.

Set in Sabon

Printed and bound in Great Britain by
CPI Group (UK) Ltd, Croydon CR0 4YY

For my parents, with love

CONTENTS

INTRODUCTION

'For us, the European Union is a means to an end – prosperity, stability, the anchor of freedom and democracy both within Europe and beyond her shores – not an end in itself. We insistently ask: How? Why? To what end?'

With these words, David Cameron introduced his plan for the next chapter of Britain's turbulent relationship with its nearest neighbours – a referendum on membership of the European Union. This book looks at the main aspects of Britain's dealings with the 28-nation organisation, the achievements and the aggravations, and asks in each case what it would mean to walk away. The pros and cons are explained in ten themes including democracy, prosperity and sovereignty, and in ten sectors where the EU most impacts everyday life in Britain such as finance, farming and fishing. Cameron proposed to reform the EU to return some of its powers back to the national level, in the hope of making it more acceptable to the British public before holding a popular vote. He made clear that his preference was to stay in the club because of the central importance of the Single Market for British businesses and British jobs. But his choice of words betrayed the ambiguity that has always characterised British involvement in Europe. The questions 'How? Why? To what end?' are a common reaction on these islands to the seemingly remorseless momentum towards further continental integration. They suggest a baffled detachment, a heavy dose of reluctance and more than a hint of suspicion.

In his announcement of Conservative plans for a referendum in 2017, known as the Bloomberg speech because it was delivered at an American financial news agency, Cameron went on to say that the EU needed to change to become more 'flexible, adaptable and open' by ditching 'spurious regulation which damages Europe's competitiveness' and to prove 'that some powers can in fact be returned to member states'. Those who suggested that meaningful reforms would simply be blocked were being 'defeatist' despite the requirement for unanimous agreement by the other twenty-seven nations for any fundamental change of the EU's ruling treaties. It was one of the most anticipated political speeches of the year and potentially one of the most significant of Cameron's premiership. It was delayed for months as the precise wording, the balance between support and criticism of the EU, and even the venue were endlessly haggled over. It was not a speech he ever wanted to make.

The Prime Minister was pushed into announcing a referendum by a large group of eurosceptic MPs in his own ranks, as well as by pressure from the media and a popular mood of disenchantment with the EU that saw a dramatic increase in support for the UK Independence

Party, a political party founded to campaign for British withdrawal from Brussels. The rise of UKIP was not just down to anger at Europe, although this was the reason it was formed at the time of the Maastricht Treaty which created the European Union. UKIP also thrived on popular anger at high levels of immigration and discontent with a political class that seemed out of touch with parts of the electorate. Nevertheless, many Conservative Party MPs felt that a referendum on EU membership would be a good way of pleasing their grass roots as well as neutralising UKIP's appeal. A referendum could also win support from voters across the political spectrum who had not had a say on Britain's relationship with Europe for four decades.

Labour avoided rushing to match Cameron's referendum promise. But in 1975 it was the Labour government of Harold Wilson that set the precedent with the country's first ballot on Europe, when the UK decided by an overwhelming two to one to stay in the European Economic Community (EEC), the forerunner of today's EU. In the depths of the Cold War and with Britain plagued by high inflation and the Three-Day Week, there was a powerful case for linking up with our continental allies. Much has changed since then. Globalisation, the fall of Communism and the emergence of developing powers like Brazil, China and India have given Britain a range of international economic options unimaginable in the 1970s. The EEC itself has been transformed, most notably by the Maastricht Treaty of 1993 that turned it into the European Union and set up the euro.

The six-nation group expanded to nine members when the UK joined in 1973 along with Denmark and Ireland, and the organisation kept growing, with the historic enlargements of 2004, 2007 and 2013 bringing eleven former Iron Curtain countries into the club. Britain was the driving force behind both the expansion and the creation of the Single Market in the 1980s which entailed abandoning the right to veto European laws in many policy areas. Further concessions of national sovereignty were made to extend EU legislative power over employment and social conditions, as well as judicial and police cooperation. The Lisbon Treaty of 2009 added the European External Action Service – the EU's own version of the Foreign Office – with branches in almost every country of the world. Public consent for these steps towards broader and deeper continental integration was never sought in a referendum – although Ireland held popular votes every time a major treaty transferred new powers to Brussels.

Frustration among the public, politicians and the media grew as the referendum option was seemingly promised by British political leaders only to be cancelled or avoided. Tony Blair said that there would be a public vote on the proposed EU Constitution in 2005, only to call it off after the French and Dutch had both voted against the document and effectively sent it back to the drawing board. Most of the proposed changes were repackaged into the Lisbon Treaty but the Labour government under Gordon Brown refused to put it to a referendum, arguing that there was no tradition for a public vote on a treaty that simply updated EU rules. Labour's argument was undermined when Valéry Giscard d'Estaing, the former French President who oversaw the drafting of the ill-fated Constitution, welcomed the Lisbon Treaty by declaring: 'The text is, in fact, a rerun of a great part of the substance of the Constitutional Treaty.' In an article in *The Sun* newspaper in 2007, David Cameron, while Leader of the Opposition, said: 'Today I will give this cast-iron guarantee: if I become PM a Conservative government will hold a referendum on any EU treaty that emerges from these negotiations.' Two years later, after the Czech Republic became the final EU country to ratify the Lisbon Treaty, Cameron, still in opposition, abandoned his referendum pledge. The changes were 'set in legal cement ... sadly our battle to stop this EU treaty has come to an end', he said.

David Cameron instinctively felt that a fight over Europe would be a diversion from his core task as Prime Minister of rebuilding the economy. That is why he told the Conservatives' annual conference in 2006 that the party needed to drop its obsession with the EU.

> For too long, instead of talking about the things that most people care about, we talked about what we cared about most. While parents worried about childcare, getting the kids to school, balancing work and family life, we were banging on about Europe.

That warning seems a long time ago now. In the same article in which he dropped his cast-iron guarantee of a referendum on the Lisbon Treaty, he admitted the real reason why he did not want to bang on about the EU: 'The to-do list for the next government is long and daunting. That is why I know that if we win that election, we cannot afford to waste time having a row with Europe.' For Cameron, Europe was not a core issue. It was a time waster. Many in his party felt differently, however, and bit by bit he was pushed into the position of announcing a referendum, even if his coalition with the pro-EU Liberal Democrats meant that he could only deliver it if re-elected in 2015 with a Conservative majority. Cameron said that he needed time for a renegotiation of the UK's terms of membership before a public vote by the end of 2017. The reason to play for time was clear – opinion polls suggested that an immediate in/out referendum would be too close to call, while a successful renegotiation could win round decisive numbers of voters.

For many years, the pro-Europeans in Britain were on the back foot as an increasingly hostile media focused relentlessly on the annoyances and absurdities of the unloved bureaucracy in Brussels. The EU gave its detractors plenty of ammunition. For the nineteenth year in a row, auditors gave an 'adverse opinion' on its accounts due to multiple 'errors' resulting in €6.7 billion being misspent in 2012 alone.[1] The crisis in the eighteen-nation eurozone highlighted the design faults in the single currency and contributed to job-destroying austerity policies in Greece, Spain, Portugal and Cyprus. These countries were all cruelly labelled 'peripheral' as the northern eurozone countries closed ranks and sought to save the currency. All the while, generous spending continued on building projects for the eurocrats, with the price tag for a gleaming new headquarters in Brussels for the President of the European Council increasing from €240 million to €327 million and the cost of the new European Central Bank building in Frankfurt doubling to at least €1.15 billion (although the bill for this one was picked up only by member states of the eurozone).[2] With the euro crisis driving several EU nations to the brink of social breakdown, there has not been much for the europhiles to shout about in recent years. In the EU's own Eurobarometer opinion poll conducted in autumn 2013, just 42 per cent of British respondents agreed that they felt 'a citizen of the EU' (the joint lowest of all twenty-eight member states along with the Greeks); only 24 per cent of the British thought 'things are going in the right direction' in the EU (joint twenty-third with the Spanish); and just 19 per cent said that they trusted the EU (only Cyprus polled lower).[3]

Nevertheless, after Cameron's Bloomberg speech in January 2013, there was a concerted pro-European fightback. This was notable among big multinational businesses which prefer the certainty of common EU rules to facilitate trade but which had kept a low profile for years in the political debate. Some of Britain's allies also voiced concerns because they value the liberalising influence of the UK upon EU rules as well as its location as a gateway to do business with the other twenty-seven member nations. New campaign groups sprang up to defend EU membership and take on the opponents of British participation who had dominated the public debate on Europe for years. There was life in the pro-EU cause after all. A real argument started about the impact of withdrawal on important areas of national life, especially immigration, trade and the City of London, as well as the environment, investment and international relations.

It was the anti-EU withdrawalists who wobbled after Cameron's speech. The prospect of a referendum exposed the lack of a clear vision about what an independent Britain would do with its new-found freedom following Brexit (British exit). Should it emulate Norway, and stay in the European Economic Area to keep full membership of the Single Market and its four freedoms of the movement of capital, goods, services and people, even though it would have no vote over the rules anymore? Should an independent Britain go back to the European Free Trade Association, which it originally helped to form in 1960 as an alternative to the EEC, and seek a series of bilateral policy agreements with the EU like Switzerland, even though the Swiss financial services sector does not enjoy complete access to the Single Market? Or should it settle for a Free Trade Agreement like a more distant partner such as South Korea or Canada? UKIP was very good at harnessing anger at the interference of the EU in everyday British life but not so good at explaining what would really happen if Britain left. The chapters of this book on the sectors most affected by the EU relationship will assess the impact of the various ways of leaving the club described above.

This book can be used as a scorecard to weigh up membership and assess whether it still works for Britain, although none of the topics exists in isolation and there are many areas of overlap, most obviously between investment and jobs or democracy and sovereignty. Not all the subjects will carry equal weight when it comes to judging the best path for Britain to follow. For some voters, the fate of British sovereignty will be far more important than the impact upon life in the City of London, while for others concerned above all about the country's balance sheet, the opposite might be the case. Nor is Britain's relationship with the EU a static one. It has changed dramatically over four decades of membership and it will keep on changing, not least as the eighteen countries in the single currency share more of their economic sovereignty to shore up the euro. Whoever wins the 2015 election, Cameron has entrenched expectations for a renegotiation of Britain's relationship and this will also change things. Some of the most important and controversial topics for the potential repatriation of powers from Brussels to the UK are discussed in the sections on immigration, employment and social conditions, justice and solidarity (regional funding).

I worked for five years in Brussels covering the EU for *The Times* before moving to Berlin to report on Germany. Angela Merkel's own arguments with Brussels and her reluctance to hand a blank cheque to the euro-zone showed that Britain was far from alone in battling with the EU. Until recently, however, Germany was the one big member state where the national consensus over the fundamental necessity for a European Union meant that there was not even a single eurosceptic political party. That changed in the 2013 election with the founding of 'Alternative für Deutschland' which called for the break-up of the euro, although not the EU itself. I confess to approaching the EU from a sceptical viewpoint – a journalistic scepticism of any system of government which spends billions of pounds of taxpayers' money. I have endeavoured to analyse the facts and test the arguments of those trying to persuade us one way or the other to stay or to leave the EU. My first book *Au Revoir, Europe,* published in December 2012, looked at how Britain reached the point of departure from the European club. This book contains the essential information and arguments for assessing what is best for Britain when it comes to deciding on Europe: in or out?

THEMES

DEMOCRACY

IN Britain, like every EU member state, has one appointed European Commissioner and one judge at the European Court of Justice. It has seventy-three out of 751 elected Members of the European Parliament (MEPs). Ministers who take decisions in meetings of the European Council must win allies to get their way under Qualified Majority Voting but have a veto in some sensitive areas like treaty change, tax, defence and foreign policy.

OUT Britain will regain control over EU policy areas but companies trading in Europe will still have to abide by standards and rules set in Brussels with no representation from UK ministers or MEPs. If the UK wants to stay in the Single Market, it must follow all the laws on the free movement of capital, goods, people and services without having a vote on them.

KEY STATS Britain's voice in the European Parliament diminished from 18.2 per cent of MEPs to 9.7 per cent as more nations joined the EU. From May 2014, it has the joint third highest number of MEPs with Italy after Germany (ninety-six) and France (seventy-four). Turnout in the 2009 European Parliament elections was 34.7 per cent in the UK compared to 65.1 per cent in the 2010 general election.

One week a month, the 751 Members of the European Parliament (MEPs), up to 2,000 staff and all their paperwork make the 250-mile trip from their offices in Brussels to their other offices in Strasbourg. Under the Treaty of Amsterdam, agreed by Sir John Major and ratified under Tony Blair, the European Parliament must meet twelve times a year in the capital of Alsace, a

German-speaking region of France chosen to symbolise
the post-war reconciliation between Europe's two great
foes. But because the parliament has a summer holiday
and does not sit in August, the whole travelling circus
by road, train and plane must take place on two separate occasions in October to make up the dozen sessions
'of equal duration' enshrined in EU law. The whole
exercise costs at least €180 million a year, meaning
that the European Parliament's seven-year budget for
2014–20 has set aside £1 billion for shuttling back and
forth between its two homes.[4] And when the European
Parliament moves, the twenty-eight members of the
European Commission also hold their weekly 'college'
meeting in Strasbourg, accompanied by their key staff.
'The current arrangements are indefensible – ludicrously
expensive and impractical. And one of the best adverts for
EU waste,' said David Lidington, the UK's Minister
for Europe. Roland Ries, the mayor of Strasbourg,
has a different view: 'The legitimacy of Strasbourg is
derived not only from law but, more importantly, from
history. As a city that symbolises Franco-German reconciliation, it is the European capital of peace, democracy
and human rights.' Holding the parliament full time
in Brussels would save 19,000 tonnes of CO_2 a year,
which would contribute to EU emissions targets.[5] MEPs
voted in 2011 to merge two of the sessions to save a
bit of money but this was immediately challenged at the
European Court of Justice by the governments of France
and Luxembourg (the Grand Duchy hosts a third site
of the European Parliament, its secretariat employing

2,432 officials). The court ruled in favour of France and Luxembourg. Then in November 2013, the democratically elected MEPs voted by 483 to 141 to base the parliament in a single location. It was a symbolic gesture. A treaty agreement can only be changed by the unanimous agreement of all member states and France would assuredly veto any attempt to end Strasbourg's special status.

Even though the European Parliament has gained new powers to amend laws with every treaty that has been passed over the last four decades, its impotence in deciding where it actually meets shows that true power in the EU machine still lies elsewhere. The member states, whose ministers and leaders meet in the European Council, remain more powerful where decisions must be made by unanimity. But their agenda is usually set by the body that proposes EU legislation – the European Commission, made up of an elite cadre of civil servants and overseen by twenty-eight nationally appointed commissioners, giving it a uniquely important role. A fourth institution, the European Court of Justice, with one appointed judge from each member state, has also become a law-making power through its many judgments over the years that have not just clarified but extended legislation. These are the four main bodies contributing to the making of EU law in a complicated system often criticised for suffering from a 'democratic deficit' and, whether the MEPs are sitting in Brussels or Strasbourg, being remote from voters.

The democratic deficit accusation partly stems from

a lack of direct consultation on the relentless development of the EU with ordinary voters who feel that they should have been offered a say through a referendum on some of the important changes, such as the creation of the European Union itself in 1993 from its predecessor, the European Community. It also arises from the system of law-making in Brussels that is hard to follow and not well understood. Senior EU figures are very touchy about claims that they lack democratic accountability, however. José Manuel Barroso, appointed President of the European Commission in 2004, used to say that he was doubly democratic because first he was elected as Prime Minister of Portugal and then he was 'elected' by the other European leaders (possibly the world's smallest constituency) to be head of the EU's bureaucracy. Every country appoints a member of the European Commission and usually it is someone who has held high political office – although Britain's last commissioner, Baroness Ashton of Upholland, was never elected to parliament having been created a life peer by Tony Blair.

But democracy can be in the eye of the beholder. It is worth pointing out that none of the 750 or so members of the House of Lords has been elected to the chamber by the public and ninety-two hereditary Lords remain on the red benches. So the UK, with its hereditary head of state, could also be said to suffer from a democratic deficit because the House of Lords has an important role in revising legislation, although the main offices of government are usually held by MPs from the elected House of Commons. The European Parliament was created to add a democratic element to a bureaucratic EU system. When Britain joined in 1973, it was a European Assembly, with thirty-six British members seconded directly from the House of Commons and House of Lords. In 1979, it held its first direct elections. Across the EU, turnout has decreased at every subsequent election from 62 per cent in 1979 to 43 per cent in 2009 (in the UK it actually went up slightly from 32.4 per cent to 34.7 per cent) suggesting that voters feel detached from a body that is poorly reported in the British media and only has the right to revise, not to propose, legislation. Few MEPs have significant recognition in Britain and it has been used as a training ground for up-and-coming Westminster politicians like Nick Clegg, who was an MEP from 1999 to 2004. The EU's own Eurobarometer poll for autumn 2013 found that only 51 per cent of British respondents even knew that Members of the European Parliament were directly elected.

As the EU has more than tripled in membership since 1973 from nine to twenty-eight nations, so has Britain's relative ability to influence its decisions – another factor in the perceived democratic deficit. The UK, especially under Tony Blair, was a champion of recruiting more eastern European countries but the result was a reduction of Britain's voting strength in the European Council from 17.2 to 8.4 per cent and in the European Parliament from 18.2 per cent of MEPs to 9.7 per cent. Even more worrying from the point of view of British influence has been the sharp drop in British officials working in the EU institutions. In 2012, only five candidates from the UK passed the tough entrance exams to work at the EU compared to seventeen from France and twenty-four from Germany. While Britain has 12.7 per cent of the EU population, the proportion of UK staff at the European Commission – the body that proposes and monitors EU laws – was down to just 4.5 per cent in 2013 compared to 8.4 per cent from Germany and 9.6 per cent from France.[6] Even Poland, which only joined the EU in 2004, supplied 4.9 per cent of EU staff. It was another aspect of Britain's growing alienation from Brussels. Bright graduates are either put off from working there by their inability to speak foreign languages or by the poor image of the EU as a place to build their careers.

Various plans have been suggested to try and address the EU's democratic deficit and to help it connect with voters. One was dreamed up by MEPs to try and boost voter turnout in the 2014 European Parliament elections – each political group agreed to nominate one prominent politician as their candidate for President of the European Commission. The theory was that linking the campaign to recognisable figures would inspire voters. There were a couple of obvious flaws in the argument – the first was the choice of uninspiring figures little known outside their own country and the second was the fact that much more recognisable figures currently running national governments were reluctant to be named as candidates for an EU position while supposedly staying focused on their day job. Two Brussels think tanks denounced the European Parliament's attempt to nominate lead candidates as 'a pretend democratic choice which could also alienate the public further' because of the risk that the candidate would ultimately be rejected by national governments anyway. 'Opponents see a vote for a Commission President via the parliament as illusory, misleading and irrelevant,' wrote *The Guardian*. 'Will a Swede vote liberal because of a Flemish contender? Or a Greek vote social democrat in support of a German? ... Or will all of them vote because of what they perceive to be going on in their own countries and politics?'

Another plan proposed by senior German politicians was to hold a direct Europe-wide election for the post of EU President, a combined role to run both the European Commission and European Council. This could see hustings held by two or three rivals in every country and would create a figure with a very powerful personal mandate to lead the EU, much like an American President. The extra authority that this would bestow on such a person makes it likely that Britain would block the proposal, as it has done in the past – not least because it would appear like a move towards a United States of Europe. That is the core issue with some of the plans to enhance the EU's direct democratic accountability – they also tend to increase its power. Besides, voters have drifted away from European Parliament elections over the years even though more responsibility has steadily been given to MEPs. It is national parliaments that should be given more say over EU legislation, according to the Fresh Start group of Conservative MPs which campaigns to curtail EU powers, in an idea taken up by the Foreign Secretary, William Hague. He floated the idea of a 'red card' that a majority of national parliaments could agree together to show to kill off a proposed EU law, extending the little-used 'yellow card' scheme to send legislation back to the European Commission for further consideration. 'Trust in the institutions is at an all-time low. The EU is facing a crisis of legitimacy,' Hague told a conference in Germany in May 2013.

> We should explore whether the yellow card provision could be strengthened or extended to give our parliaments the right to ask the Commission to start again where legislation is too intrusive, and fails the proportionality test. And we should think about going further still and consider a red card to give national parliaments the right to block legislation that need not be agreed at the European level.

Cameron has hinted that he supports this idea, saying in his Bloomberg speech that, 'It is national parliaments which are, and will remain, the true source of real democratic legitimacy and accountability in the EU... We need to recognise that in the way the EU does business.' Of course, national politicians are bound to say that – but MPs are much closer to the electorate and therefore more likely to be in tune with voters' demands.

The 'yellow card' was introduced by the Lisbon Treaty in 2009 but is viewed as weak because it only allows national parliaments to ask the Commission to 'reconsider' a proposal. It was only used twice up until the end of 2013. In the second case, on the proposed European Public Prosecutor, the European Commission decided to go ahead regardless, despite the opposition of eleven national parliaments. This prompted the Fresh Start group to go even further in their proposals, suggesting that 'a real game changer for democratic accountability' would be to allow the red card to apply to existing rules and not just new proposals.

> This would at last provide a mechanism for national parliaments to tackle existing, poor legislation and would provide a permanent means to reverse the ongoing EU power-grab. The Dutch Parliament recently proposed a similar mechanism. A red card on existing legislation should trigger a one-year sunset clause after which the legislation would expire unless particular member states decide to retain it under enhanced cooperation among themselves.

This kind of proposal is likely to be rejected out of hand across the EU, given its potential to unravel the whole enterprise, which is based upon all member states agreeing to honour past agreements – even when the governments that made those agreements change. John Bruton, the former Irish Taoiseach, said in December 2013 that the red card proposal would paralyse EU decision-making. 'Does it [Britain] want the European Union to continue – whether it is in it or not – as a workable entity that has the capacity to make decisions reasonably efficiently, or does it want the European Union essentially to wither away?' Making the 'red card' one of Britain's conditions for staying in the EU during a renegotiation of the relationship in the run-up to a referendum could result in rejection by the other member states, pushing the UK towards the exit. Yet even this idea did not go far enough for ninety-five Conservative MPs, who were said to have signed a letter to David Cameron in January 2014 calling for national parliaments to have the individual right of a red card veto over EU laws. William Hague spelled out why giving single parliaments the right of veto was incompatible with membership of the EU:

> If parliaments all around the EU were regularly and unilaterally able to choose which bits of EU law they would apply and which bits they would not, the European Single Market would not work and even a Swiss-style free trade arrangement with the EU would not work.

It was a sign of how strongly the ninety-five Conservative MPs felt about returning the UK Parliament's democratic supremacy that they proposed a measure which would unravel the EU and wreck even the Single Market created by Margaret Thatcher, seen as the most important part of the EU by other Conservatives.

Leaving the EU would not necessarily resolve the democratic deficit felt by many in Britain. Under one scenario, it could even get worse. An option for Britain if it took the democratic decision in a referendum to leave the EU would be to follow non-members Norway, Iceland and Liechtenstein into the European Economic Area (EEA) to preserve full access to the Single Market. Unlike full EU members, the EEA countries make their own policies on farming, fishing, justice, overseas trade and regional funding but are duty bound to accept every EU law relating to the four freedoms – the movement of capital, goods, people and services – that underpin the Single Market. That includes accepting all the EU's social and employment legislation along with state aid, competition and consumer protection laws which are regarded by Brussels as integral to the Single Market system, as well as most of its environmental laws. As an EU member, Britain has been able to block the full force of the EU Working Time Directive by finding allies to support an opt-out from its 48-hour week. If Britain left the EU, the blocking alliance could crumble, leaving the UK legally required to implement the directive in full if it joined the EEA to stay inside the Single Market – a policy estimated at costing British employers between £9.2 and 11.9 billion a year.[7] The EEA members also accept the free movement of workers on the same basis as EU members and with the same access to national welfare systems.

An independent review for the Norwegian government concluded in 2012 that a democratic deficit was inevitable if Norway took part in the Single Market but not the EU:

The most problematic aspect of Norway's form of association with the EU is the fact that Norway is in practice
bound to adopt EU policies and rules on a broad range
of issues without being a member and without voting
rights. This raises democratic problems. Norway is not
represented in decision-making processes that have direct
consequences for Norway, and neither do we have any
significant influence on them. Moreover, our form of
association with the EU dampens political engagement
and debate in Norway and makes it difficult to monitor
the Government and hold it accountable in its European
policy. This is not surprising; the democratic deficit is a
well-known aspect of the EEA Agreement that has been
there from the start. It is the price Norway pays for
enjoying the benefits of European integration without
being a member of the organisation that is driving these
developments.

Norway's Conservative Prime Minister, Erna Solberg,
warned Britain against following her country into the
EEA relationship with the EU. Ahead of talks with
Cameron in 2014, she said:

I don't believe that Great Britain, with its old empire
mind-set, should consider becoming a member of an
organisation which basically means that laws and rules
which are made in other countries are implemented
directly. I think those in the British debate who look
at Norway's association underestimate how closely

connected we actually are with many of the laws and rules they are annoyed with.

Switzerland also refused to join the EU and rejected the EEA in a referendum in 1992 to stay in the European Free Trade Association (EFTA) outside the Single Market. It has a Free Trade Agreement for goods but not for services, and has agreed around 200 technical bilateral agreements on different aspects of cooperation, from research to transport. Nevertheless, it effectively adopts large swathes of EU law to maintain its strong trading links (64.7 per cent of total Swiss trade was with the EU in 2012[8]) and its involvement in the Schengen borderless travel zone which means Switzerland has done away with passport checks for those entering from the EU. Britain has not joined the Schengen system. 'In order to make its economy as EU-compatible as possible, Switzerland has adopted a policy of "voluntary adaptation" whereby Swiss law is aligned with the EU's acquis communautaire [body of law],' said the Centre for Swiss Politics at the University of Kent, in a paper for MPs' Foreign Affairs Select Committee.

Recent research shows that around 55 per cent of the laws passed by the Swiss parliament concern transposition of international, including EU, law. The bilateral treaties and the country's voluntary adaptation have led to Switzerland being much more deeply integrated with the EU than suggested by its formal status as a non-member. Indeed, in certain respects such integration is deeper than that of EU members such as the UK, as the case of Schengen shows.

The Swiss system offers a more democratic solution than the Norwegian model because all new laws are scrutinised by its parliament, although many are of EU origin. Switzerland does retain, on paper at least, full legal decision-making powers over the laws it passes. It does not fall under the jurisdiction of the European Court of Justice. Another attraction of the Swiss model for those who want Britain to withdraw from the EU is the fact that it does not have to implement Single Market legislation relating to social and employment law.

Senior figures in the EU are painfully aware that they are regarded as remote, unrecognised and undemocratic. Nearly a quarter of British people (23 per cent) told the autumn 2013 Eurobarometer poll that they had not even heard of the European Parliament and 29 per cent said they had not heard of the European Commission. If nothing else, it was an indictment of schools, the media and politicians themselves for failing to communicate the basic structures of the EU. Faced with growing levels of discontent across the EU, the Lisbon Treaty proposed a measure called the European Citizens' Initiative to try and make a direct connection with voters. This requires the European Commission to consider proposing legislation if called upon by a petition signed by at least one million people from at least one quarter of the member states. It was partly inspired by the earlier petition to end the European Parliament's travelling circus which gained 1.27 million signatures (although it has not yet achieved its aim). The first completed petition under the new scheme, for 'water as a human right', recorded 1.65 million verified signatures and was handed to the European Commission in January 2014 demanding 'legislation implementing the human right to water and sanitation as recognised by the United Nations, and promoting the provision of water and sanitation as essential public services for all'. A campaign to do away with animal experimentation and another to end the EU funding of research using human embryos have also gathered the requisite signatures, although a petition to phase out nuclear energy was rejected, as this was deemed not within the power of the EU. It remains to be seen what action will be taken on successful petitions – and whether this form of direct democracy does anything at all to improve the popular legitimacy of the institutions in Brussels (and Strasbourg). But the European Citizens' Initiative seems more like a small sticking plaster on the very real sense of democratic detachment felt by voters in many European countries between themselves and the EU.

DIPLOMACY AND BRITAIN'S PLACE IN THE WORLD

IN Britain uses its influence in the EU to try and make it more competitive, while foreign policy goals can be enhanced through the collective strength of the twenty-eight member nations in trade talks or other 'soft power' actions such as aid or sanctions on rogue regimes and the response to crises and natural disasters.

OUT Britain can develop new global allegiances through its trans-Atlantic and Commonwealth links, build on its close military cooperation with France and remain a key member of NATO and many other international bodies such as the G8 and G20. It can take its own seat on the World Trade Organization.

KEY STATS The UK has the second highest number of Nobel Prize winners, is the world's fourth biggest military spender, the fifth largest importer, has the sixth highest GDP and is one of five permanent members of the United Nations Security Council.

Vladimir Putin's spokesman touched a raw British nerve when he was quoted declaring that, 'Britain is just a small island ... no one pays any attention to them apart from the Russian oligarchs who have bought up Chelsea.' The taunt at the G20 summit in St Petersburg followed David Cameron's call for military intervention in Syria over its use of chemical weapons – even though the House of Commons had voted against involvement. Putin, the Russian President, was also opposed. Not surprisingly, the reported Russian remark triggered British tabloid outrage and a robust response from the Prime Minister. 'Britain may be a small island, but I would challenge anyone to find a country with a prouder history, a bigger heart or greater resilience,' Cameron said.

> Britain is an island that has helped to clear the European continent of fascism... Britain is an island that helped to abolish slavery, that has invented most of the things worth inventing, including every sport currently played around the world. We are very proud of everything we do as a small island – a small island that has the sixth largest economy, the fourth best funded military, some of the most effective diplomats, the proudest history, one of the best records for art and literature and contribution to philosophy and world civilisation.

Later, at his press conference, Cameron added an important footnote. 'Our music delights and amuses millions, The Beatles, Elgar and ... One Direction have conquered the world.' It was certainly a proud record compared to most countries, including Russia – best known for giving the world Communism, vodka and oligarchs – and which has yet to produce anything in pop music to better The Beatles. Or even One Direction. Moscow officially denied the 'small island' comment, which was allegedly made in a private briefing for Russian journalists. But the controversy came at a sensitive time, with Britain's place in the front rank of world affairs seemingly vulnerable to the rise of developing nations as well as belt-tightening at the Foreign Office and Armed Forces – the full-time British Army head count is being reduced from 102,000 to 82,000. The minimum number of Royal Navy frigates and destroyers thought to be necessary to assure national security in 1998 was thirty-two, was reduced to twenty-five in 2004 amid cost savings and has fallen to nineteen today.[9] MPs on the Foreign Affairs Select Committee warned in January 2014 that the Foreign Office was 'being stretched, almost to the limit' and 'may be in danger of trying to do too much at a time when capacity is being limited' with targets for a 10 per cent cut in UK-based staff by 2015. At the same time as all these cutbacks, the EU has been developing its own overseas representation and presence on the global stage through the European External Action Service created in the Lisbon Treaty of 2009. In December 2013, it had 1,498 staff in Brussels and 1,869 more in 139 delegation offices around the world, while its 2014 draft budget was €518,628,447.[10]

A couple of former Prime Ministers were among the prominent British and foreign leaders and diplomats who were prompted by Cameron's pledge of an EU referendum to come out and warn that Britain's 'position in the world' would suffer by voting to leave. Sir John Major said that 'it would be folly beyond belief, in a world of seven billion people who are binding more closely together, for brave little Blighty to decide she is suddenly going to … cut off Europe in a thick fog and decide to go on her own.' Tony Blair said:

When people say it is debatable whether leaving would mean that Britain had less influence in the world, it really isn't. Anyone who has held the office of Prime Minister knows that our position within the EU is absolutely central to our position in the world. The idea that we would form equal relationships with China and India with an identity separate from the EU is risible to anyone who has seen how big power politics works. On areas such as trade, EU membership gives us huge commercial advantages. And in the political arenas like the G8 and G20, Britain has far greater heft because we are alongside other EU nations.

Blair knows more than most about the world stage. He ensured that Britain stayed close to the US despite tensions with fellow Europeans – but his decision to go to war in Iraq in 2003 split the EU down the middle and led Gerhard Schroeder, the German Chancellor, to despair that Europe could ever have a meaningful common foreign policy.

Even Cameron, who had criticised several aspects of the EU, was absolutely clear that Britain's place in the world was enhanced by membership. 'We would have to think carefully too about the impact on our influence at the top table of international affairs,' he said in his Bloomberg speech.

There is no doubt that we are more powerful in Washington, in Beijing, in Delhi because we are a powerful player in the European Union. That matters for British jobs and British security. It matters to our ability to get things done in the world. It matters to the United States and other friends around the world, which is why many tell us very clearly that they want Britain to remain in the EU. We should think very carefully before giving that position up.

It was a clear sign that Cameron believed Britain should stay in.

As one of the few EU members which considers itself an active player on the stage of world diplomacy, Britain has been able to harness EU structures to extend its own foreign policy goals, notably through the added clout of joint sanctions against regimes like those in Iran and Zimbabwe. Rogue leaders like Robert Mugabe and his entourage are stung far more by the loss of travel and banking rights or weapons embargoes in twenty-eight countries than in one. That is why Lord Wright of Richmond, Head of the Diplomatic Service from 1986 to 1991, said that 'it has sometimes been argued that British diplomacy boxes above our weight. Surely, departure from the EU would deprive us of the major ring in which to box?' Another of the country's foremost foreign affairs commentators, Robin Niblett, director of the Chatham House think tank, declared that Britain had an important role to play in the EU in

liberalising the single market, reforming the EU budget, promoting a more interconnected EU energy market, striking trade agreements with increasingly assertive emerging powers, and implementing powerful EU sanctions regimes against countries such as Syria and Iran. The idea that a British government can deliver a better future for its citizens sitting outside these areas of EU decision-making than it can inside is fanciful.

Two former ambassadors to Washington, both appointed by Blair, joined the chorus of leading diplomatic figures concerned with the potential loss of influence in the so-called special relationship with the US if Britain left the EU.

Sir David Manning, Blair's former foreign policy advisor and ambassador to Washington from 2003 to 2007, claimed that America looked to the EU as its 'natural partner' and believed that Britain's role was enhanced as a member. 'Outside the EU, our influence in Europe would be sharply diminished – but so it would be in the United States. The risk to the UK of leaving the European Union is of a rapid drift into international irrelevance,' he said.

Compelling economic arguments are made for the UK's membership of the European Union, not least the importance of the single market in which we do almost half our trade. But equally compelling are the strategic, security and diplomatic interests served by UK membership, interests that would be seriously jeopardised were we to leave the EU.

Manning's successor in Washington, Sir Nigel Sheinwald, who was formerly ambassador to the EU, gave his own warning about the impact of Brexit on Britain's foreign and defence policy:

> On foreign and defence issues, we can exert greater traction globally for our positions when they are backed by the rest of the EU. That's why William Hague, a long-standing critic of the EU's internal processes, nevertheless sees the importance of EU-wide agreement when something needs to be done, for example, on Syria, Egypt, Zimbabwe or Burma.

Support for British membership of the EU came from the very top of the US government during the debate about Cameron's referendum proposal. Joe Biden, the vice-president, told *The Times*: 'We believe the United Kingdom is stronger as a result of its membership. And we believe the EU is stronger with the UK's involvement. That's our view.' President Obama himself also weighed in, declaring in a White House statement that 'the United States values a strong UK in a strong European Union, which makes critical contributions to peace, prosperity, and security in Europe and around the world'. But this was not the unanimous view of American politicians. Speaking in December 2013 in London, Marco Rubio, a Republican senator for Florida seen as a potential presidential candidate, called the special relationship between Britain and the US 'unshakable' whatever happened in an EU referendum. 'As for Britain's role in Europe, that should be a matter for the British people to decide and for your American partners to respect whatever decision you make,' he said. 'Our alliance, our partnership and our affection for your nation will continue regardless of the road you choose.' Here, he was echoing a strand of Republican thinking that led the Speaker of the House of Representatives, Newt Gingrich, to state in 1998 that, 'If, as appears likely, there is a movement in the US Congress, as there has been in the Parliament of Canada, to offer Britain some associate status in the North America Free Trade Agreement, I would support it.' This was simply not possible while Britain remained a member of the EU because the power to conduct trade negotiations is one that all EU member states hand over to the bureaucrats in Brussels. Whether or not Gingrich was aware of that, the American reaction showed a tendency for the US to split on party lines over the necessity for Britain to stay in the EU, mirroring the position in the UK itself. John Bolton, a staunch Republican who was US Ambassador to the United Nations under President George W. Bush, wrote that:

The State Department should remember that Thomas Jefferson, its first Secretary, once wrote: 'It cannot be to our interest that all Europe should be reduced to a single monarchy.' ... Until America once again has a president prepared to deal effectively with global threats to US interests, there is obviously little that those of us in opposition can do to support a United Kingdom determined to preserve some measure of democratic sovereignty. But rest assured, you are far better off making up your own minds than having Barack Obama make them up for you.

European leaders want Britain to stay in the EU because of the extra strength this gives to the organisation on the world stage – as well as the extra cash from Britain's net contribution and its strong liberalising influence around the table. José Manuel Barroso went further and warned that the UK's own prestige would suffer if it left. 'From a European perspective, I find it a little bit ironic that some people are suggesting for Britain a role comparable to that of, say, Norway or Switzerland,' he said.

'The fact that some are suggesting for Britain a role that is smaller than the one Britain already has today seems to me a little bit curious.' Barroso said that when David Cameron met President Obama, he had 'much stronger leverage because everybody knows that Britain is a country that is very influential in the shaping of Europe'. While British politicians avoided criticising Obama and Biden for their interventions, they readily attacked Barroso. Martin Callanan, leader of the European Conservative MEPs in the European Parliament, said:

It is precisely because Britain is such an international-ist country that it does not wish to become just another state in a federal Europe. Britain has its own ties and relationships with the rest of the world. Barroso has become so blinkered about his European project that the idea of a large country standing on its own two feet eludes him. Britain can have a much looser relationship with the EU and still extend its influence in the world. When Cameron visits Washington, he does so as the leader of the USA's most reliable partner and longest-standing international ally, not as just another EU leader.

Nor should Barroso simply be allowed to trash the global influence of Norway, which for a country of just five million maintains a formidable humanitarian reputation, taking a leading role in peace and reconciliation talks in the Middle East (leading to the Oslo Accords), Colombia, Haiti, the Philippines, Somalia, Sri Lanka and Uganda. Switzerland is the location for numerous world bodies such as the Red Cross, World Trade Organization, UN High Commissioner for Refugees and World Economic Forum, and it played host to the 2014 Syrian peace talks.

Cameron has made a strong case for continued EU membership alongside Britain's participation in a number of international forums. In so doing, he highlighted the number of different stages on which Britain plays out its global role.

> We are playing our part to build a world that is more stable and more ordered, because it is right in itself and because it is in our own enlightened national interest. Another key part of that effort is our place in international organisations. At the UN. The Commonwealth. NATO. The WTO. The G8. The G20. And, yes, the EU. Membership of these organisations is not national vanity – it is in our national interest.

Strangely he included the World Trade Organization among the bodies where the UK wields influence, even though belonging to the EU denies Britain its own seat at the table – an oversight immediately spotted by the UK Independence Party. 'It is hard to tell if the Prime Minister is being ignorant or dishonest when he claims that Britain is at the top table at the WTO. We are not,' said Nigel Farage, the UKIP leader.

> We are represented only through the EU and its trade commissioner. Only if we left the EU could Britain be a true member of the WTO. Independence would mean greater, not lesser influence on the world stage. Likewise, Mr Cameron knows that Britain's membership in the Commonwealth, the G8, the G20 and NATO would be completely unaffected by leaving the EU. He also knows that our permanent membership of the UN Security Council is actually threatened by our continued membership of the EU, which wants a larger role for itself at the UN.

An independent Britain would indeed claim its own seat at the WTO alongside the other 158 members, the size of the body making this more of a symbolic sign of freedom from the EU. Farage was right, however, to raise concerns about the long-term status of Britain's seat on the UN Security Council, where since the end of the Second World War it has been one of five permanent members alongside China, France, Russia and the United States. This is clearly a major source of the UK's international prestige and – whatever one thinks of the UN's effectiveness – places Britain firmly in the first rank of nations globally. A recurring theme of reform plans for the permanent membership is not only to bring in a country from Africa, South America and possibly also India, but also to consolidate the European representation as an EU seat. There would be less logic behind this if Britain left the EU and therefore also its Common Foreign and Security Policy (CFSP) run by its European External Action Service. And despite Blair's assertion that 'anyone who has held the office of Prime Minister knows that our position within the EU is absolutely central to our position in the world', we learned in 2013 that this did not apply to everyone who occupied Number 10. There was one Prime Minister who concluded that Britain would be better off out of the EU – and it was the Prime Minister credited with enhancing the country's global position through cementing a close relationship with the US and acting decisively with military force when circumstances demanded. Margaret Thatcher came to believe that Britain should quit the EU, according to her biographer Charles Moore.

Andrew Neil interviewed me about my biography of Margaret Thatcher. He asked me if, after leaving office, Lady Thatcher had come to the view that Britain should leave the European Union. I said yes (I think it happened after the Maastricht Treaty in 1992), although advisers had persuaded her that she should not say this in public

since it would have allowed her opponents to drive her
to the fringes of public life.

Times have changed considerably since voicing a desire
to quit the EU was felt to be beyond the pale in polite
society, however, with even the Chancellor of the
Exchequer George Osborne and other Conservative
Cabinet ministers stating openly in 2014 that Britain
could leave unless the EU was reformed.

The revelation about Thatcher showed that opinion is
divided over whether Britain needs to remain in the EU
to project itself on the world stage. It is divided between
British Prime Ministers and between senior American
politicians. But the divide is split on party lines and
the weight of opinion is in favour of EU membership.
The overwhelming majority of senior diplomats, who
perhaps have much to lose through Brexit, believe
Britain should stay in the Brussels club to try and make
it work better and also to use it to enhance the country's
well-established global presence. In the future, economic
'soft power' such as sanctions, trade and development
aid will be the key to successful international diplomacy
as much as the 'hard power' of military might. The
constant struggle to remain relevant and influential in
a rapidly changing world was shown by an editorial
in China's nationalistic *Global Times* tabloid, which
welcomed Cameron on a visit to the capital in 2013 by
writing that: 'The UK is not a big power in the eyes of
the Chinese. It is just an old European country apt for

travel and study.' Britain does still command widespread respect through its impressive achievements as listed by Cameron in response to the earlier Russian jibe but, if it did leave the EU, it would need to work harder to maintain its clout in Beijing and Moscow, not to mention Washington and Brussels.

IMMIGRATION

IN Free movement of workers between the twenty-eight EU countries is one of the four core principles of the Single Market along with the free movement of capital, goods and services. Any EU citizen can come to Britain with their family to work, use schools and the NHS and receive welfare benefits, if they pass an habitual residence test; Britons are able to enjoy the same rights in other EU countries.

OUT Britain could regain the right to turn away EU citizens at its border and could bring in an Australian-style immigration system, only allowing long-term access to those with shortage skills, like nurses, or seasonal workers on temporary visas. In this case, UK citizens might face reciprocal difficulties living and working in EU countries.

KEY STATS 7.7 million foreign-born people including 2.6 million EU-born citizens live in the UK of whom 700,000 are Polish;[11] 2.2 million Britons live in other EU countries including a million in Spain.[12] The Home Office has no figures on the number of EU 'benefit tourists' who came for hand-outs. Polling shows that 77 per cent of Britons want fewer immigrants and 56 per cent want the number to be 'a lot' lower.[13]

Amid the political and media frenzy over the lifting of all restrictions on Bulgarians and Romanians coming to the UK in 2014, it was a Hungarian who upset the British government the most by declaring that David Cameron's 'unilateral rhetoric [on limiting unemployment benefits to EU migrants] is not really helpful, because it risks presenting the UK as a nasty country in the European Union. We don't want that.' The Hungarian was László Andor, who represented his country as the European Commissioner for Employment, Social Affairs and Inclusion. This was an echo of the warning given to the Conservative Party to modernise back in 2002, when Theresa May, then chair of the party, said: 'You know what some people call us? The nasty party.' Her goal was to startle the Conservatives into adopting more socially aware policies and appeal to a wider range of voters. Andor seemed to suggest that the Conservatives had not changed one bit. As a Socialist and an Anglophile who studied in the UK and spent five years working in London, he knew how to needle David Cameron, who took the bait. The Prime Minister told Twitter that he had complained to Andor's boss, José Manuel Barroso: 'I raised Commissioner Andor's comments with @BarrosoEU – totally inappropriate for unelected officials to complain about legitimate concerns.' It was hardly a convincing response by Cameron, complaining that the European Commission was unelected and then protesting to another of its unelected officials. It was left up to William Hague, the Foreign Secretary, to give a more effective reply, declaring:

> We have to make it clear, and other European countries want to make it clear, that where there is an entitlement to free movement for work across the European Union, that is for work, it is not for claiming the benefits of another country. We are well within our rights to make

that clear. There is nothing nasty about that. This is not just Britain being awkward in Europe; this is Britain giving voice to many people in Europe who say that freedom of movement for work is for work, not to claim more generous benefits in another country.

This went straight to the heart of an issue that in 2013 became the key focus of discontent in Britain with the European Union. Immigration had become the number one rallying cry of the UK Independence Party and – on the flimsiest of evidence – senior Conservative members of the coalition government tried to outdo each other with policy promises to give the impression of taking action on the hot issue of the day.

With its campaign against the right of Bulgarians and Romanians to live and work in the UK under the EU's Freedom of Movement Directive, UKIP ruthlessly exposed the glaring inconsistency in David Cameron's attitude towards Brussels. The Prime Minister spent years praising the Single Market as the EU's most valuable asset, citing it as the main reason for remaining a member even as he prepared the conditions for a referendum that could see Britain leave. But the Single Market is not just about trade. The so-called four freedoms – of goods, capital, labour and services – are its four cornerstones and have been since Margaret Thatcher did so much to help set up the Single Market in the 1980s. Cameron could not claim to support the system without defending the right to the free movement of people looking for work. However, the Prime Minister also wanted to appeal to UKIP supporters by sounding tough on the aspect of Europe that most annoyed many people – the policy that encouraged wholesale migration. This was helpfully summed up in November 2013 by Viviane Reding, a vice president of the European Commission: 'If Britain wants to leave the Single Market you should say so. If Britain wants to stay a part of the Single Market, free movement applies. You cannot have your cake and eat it, Mr Cameron.' From the opposite corner, Nigel Farage, leader of the UK Independence Party, spelled out why, when appealing to voters whose top concern is immigration, Cameron could never beat UKIP's promise to leave the EU:

This is the man who throughout his whole leadership of the Conservative Party has said that free movement of people is an essential part of the Single Market; he has been the biggest cheerleader in Brussels for the EU expanding, to take in not just Turkey but the Ukraine. Membership of the European Union means you have lost control of your borders. It is that simple.

Unable to do much about migration from current EU states, Cameron's policy response was to argue that countries joining in the future should face restrictions on the free movement of their citizens until their GDP exceeds a certain level, even though the prospect of new member states arriving was some years off.

EU citizens – a status created in the Maastricht Treaty of 1993 that was agreed by Conservative Prime Minister

John Major – have the right to free movement to look for work as a condition of membership of the EU. One important thing that has changed enormously since Britain joined the six original EEC members in 1973 – and even since the time of Maastricht when there were still only twelve members – is the dramatic enlargement of the EU to include countries with much poorer economies than Britain's. Free movement made perfect sense when all the member countries had broadly comparable living standards and earning expectations. But UK GDP per capita is three times what it is in Bulgaria, Romania and Croatia, the most recent countries to join the EU with a combined population of 33 million, bringing membership to twenty-eight nations and 504 million people. It is small wonder that politicians in other member states were taken aback by the vehemence of the British political and media outcry over the lifting of restrictions on Bulgarians and Romanians when the UK had been the most active and outspoken campaigner for more and more nations to join. Such was the British government's enthusiasm for new members that Labour ministers regarded it as almost rude to suggest that they should make use of temporary limits on migration from the eight former Communist countries that joined in 2004. 'It is important that we send as positive a signal as possible – not just as a government, but as a whole Parliament – to all the acceding countries,' Beverley Hughes, then Immigration Minister, told the House of Commons in June 2003 while making the case against limiting arrivals from the new member states including

Poland, Hungary and the Czech Republic. It would make them 'second-class citizens', she added. 'It is our position that the government should extend to these countries the hand of friendship.' This completely ignored the fact that Britain used temporary restrictions for six years to control migrants from the previous accessions of Greece, Portugal and Spain. It also overlooked the fact that Germany and Austria kept controls on workers from Eastern Europe for the full seven years allowed under EU rules, without suffering a loss of friendship with Poland or their other neighbours.

The Home Office had commissioned independent research from University College London that predicted the number of permanent migrants from the ten new countries would be between 5,000 and 13,000 a year. In fairness, the authors warned that there would be more if other countries had safeguards, which they did, while Britain had none. But it was still dramatically wrong. An average of 170,000 long-term migrants – those staying more than twelve months – came every year from 2004 to 2011. As Labour began to distance itself from the high immigration years of its time in office, Jack Straw, who was Foreign Secretary at the time the new EU countries joined, admitted in November 2013 that failing to apply transitional restrictions on Eastern European migrants was a 'spectacular mistake'. Writing in the *Lancashire Telegraph*, he added that 'net migration reached close to a quarter of a million at its peak in 2010. Lots of red faces, mine included.'

The damage was huge, not only to the government's

reputation and the reliability of political assurances about the EU but also in the erosion of traditional British tolerance of newcomers. The most noticeable of these were Roma, with an estimated 200,000 in the UK by 2013, making it one of the largest communities of its kind in Europe.[14] This led to an even more alarming warning from David Blunkett, the man who oversaw the open-door policy to new EU citizens as Labour's Home Secretary. 'Many of them don't even live in areas where there are toilets or refuse collection facilities,' he said in November 2013. 'We have got to change the behaviour and the culture of the incoming community, the Roma community, because there's going to be an explosion otherwise. We all know that.'

A better way to respond to the exaggerated fears of the numbers who might come flocking over from these countries would be to point to some basic facts about EU migration. Eastern Europeans coming to Britain are generally younger and more economically active than the average person in the host population, and there was 'little evidence' that so-called benefits tourism motivated them to move to countries with generous welfare payments, a study by the European Commission said in 2013. Healthcare and benefits costs associated with new arrivals from the former Communist countries remained 'very low', it concluded – despite estimating that the additional burden on the NHS was between €1.1 billion and €1.8 billion in 2011 alone. That amounted to 1.1 per cent of health expenditure in Britain. But the report suggested that the economic contribution of the migrants far exceeded these social costs. That was because only 30 per cent of EU migrants in Britain were 'economically inactive' – defined as students, pensioners, job-seekers or home-makers – compared with 43 per cent of the wider British population. Unemployment among EU migrants in the UK was 7.5 per cent, compared with 7.9 per cent among Britons in 2012. Moreover, the government has had an habitual residence test since 1994, strengthened in 2004 with a 'right to reside' test, to weed out benefit claimants with no ties to the UK. Nevertheless, Theresa May, now Home Secretary, insisted that some European migrants abused the EU's free movement laws to become an 'unacceptable burden' as so-called benefit tourists. Despite repeated requests for evidence from the European Commission, May's department offered no figures to back up her claims. 'Finland, Sweden, Germany or the UK did not comment on this matter due to lack of evidence,' the authors of the migrant study noted. May warned during her 'nasty party' speech in 2002 that 'some Tories have tried to make political capital by demonising minorities instead of showing confidence in all the citizens of our country'. A decade later and without detailed evidence, she accused EU migrants in Britain of abusing the welfare state. There were individual cases of fraud, such as that of Lavinia Olmazu, who helped 172 Romanians illegally claim £2.9 million in benefits after becoming a campaigner for the rights of Roma and was jailed for two years and three months. But it was hard for the Home Office to compete more generally on facts because it simply did not collect data on which European nationalities abused welfare benefits.

The Department for Work and Pensions did compile a report on estimated work-related benefit claims by different nationalities. From an analysis of National Insurance numbers, it found that 5.76 million people were claiming working age benefits in 2011 in Britain, of whom 371,100 were non-UK nationals (6.4 per cent). Of these, 91,310 were from EU countries (1.6 per cent of claimants) including 28,740 from the twelve mainly Eastern European countries that joined after 2004 (0.5 per cent of all benefit claimants in the UK). There were more benefit claimants from Africa (97,760) and from Asia and the Middle East (125,690) than from the entire EU. Country by country, the table of foreign benefit claimants was headed by those born in Pakistan (33,060), then Somalia (25,480) with India in third place (19,380). There were six EU nations in the top twenty countries of UK benefit claimants, led by Ireland in fourth place (15,630) and followed by Poland in seventh place (13,940 or 0.24 per cent of all claimants). These figures suggested that very few EU citizens could be 'benefit tourists'. They showed that Europe was the source of less than one-third of foreign benefit claimants in Britain. In December 2013, following the media outcry over the lifting of work restrictions on Bulgarians and Romanians, the government added more questions to the habitual residence test and announced that EU migrants would not be able to claim Jobseeker's Allowance until they had been resident for three months. New claims would be limited in most cases to six months' duration.

An independent Britain, after leaving the EU, could impose strict immigration rules like Australia, which only allows long-term access to students, family members and those with skills required in the country. Campaigners for Britain to leave the EU, such as the Conservative MEP David Campbell Bannerman, have argued that the UK could then do bilateral deals for visa-free access with those European economies of a similar size like France and Italy. The problems would start if the EU closed ranks against the UK and insisted on an 'all or nothing' approach to the Schengen zone of twenty-six countries which have abolished internal passport controls. While this does not yet include Bulgaria and Romania, it does cover poorer countries like Poland and Greece. If an independent Britain failed to establish a visa-free arrangement with Spain, for example, home to a million British citizens, then retiring to the Costas could become much more bureaucratic. Spain might not be well disposed to forming good bilateral relations with Britain if it left the EU, or could perhaps use the issue as a bargaining chip over the future sovereignty of Gibraltar. Non-EU migrants to Spain have to fill out much more paperwork, for example criminal record checks and certificates of tax status, while they also have to take the Spanish driving test if they want to own a car, unlike EU citizens whose driving licence is mutually recognised. Moreover, the skills that Britain needs from immigrants are not confined to certain nationalities. Sir James Dyson, the vacuum cleaner entrepreneur, gave a glimpse of how tighter controls on immigration were already affecting engineering when he threatened in February 2014 to leave the UK unless more was done to retain foreign engineering students when they graduate. He warned that 61,000 vacancies would remain unfilled through a combination of a lack of home-grown engineers and foreign students unwilling – or unable – to stay. Employers faced an 'avalanche of paperwork' to keep them on and they were often only allowed a fixed-term contract. 'The reason these engineers go home is because we do everything we can to make them unwelcome,' he told the *Financial Times*.

Britain would also suffer if it withdrew from the Dublin Convention, an EU system for returning asylum-seekers to the country where they first entered the EU and which benefits the UK because many first cross into Europe through southern border states like Greece or Italy.

No other area of EU policy is as fraught with confusion, misinformation and hyperbole as immigration. The ridiculously low estimate of new arrivals from the former Communist countries after 2004 was typical of this. The Labour government was ideologically predisposed to play down the size of the likely influx and the associated social problems. When the independent study commissioned by the Home Office came up with a prediction of 5,000 to 13,000 arrivals every year, a Labour MEP, Claude Moraes, angrily challenged the forecast as 'far too high', arguing that when poorer countries like Portugal joined before there was 'virtually no immigration'. Newspapers on either side of the debate played their usual roles: the headline in *The*

Guardian on the forecast was 'Expansion of EU will not mean more immigration' while in the *Daily Express* it was 'Britain faces flood of new immigrants'. Ten years later, similar exaggerations were apparent on both sides of the argument over Bulgarians and Romanians gaining full freedom to live and work in Britain. This time they were exacerbated by the tougher economic climate and the challenge posed by UKIP to the Conservatives in the opinion polls. Opposition to immigration was fuelled by claims that it drove down wages and deprived British workers of jobs. Yet the Organisation for Economic Cooperation and Development has concluded that a direct link between immigration and the loss of jobs among the host population is hard to prove over the long term.

An increase in the share of immigrants in the labour force increases unemployment of natives, but this impact is temporary and vanishes between four and nine years after the shock. Beyond this transitory period, the level of the share of immigrants in the labour force does not influence significantly natives' unemployment.

That is the dry economic conclusion but the wider social and cultural impact of immigration means that many voters will make it their top priority in the promised referendum on EU membership.

Britain can only regain full control over who enters the country by quitting the EU. UKIP is therefore bound to win the argument over how to regain ultimate sovereignty over Britain's borders, no matter how many new ways the government dreams up to make life in Britain a bit more difficult for Bulgarians and Romanians. If the UK was to leave but then follow non-member Norway into the European Economic Area in order to stay in the Single Market, the government would still be duty bound to follow the market's four freedoms including the freedom of movement of workers. Even Switzerland, which lies outside the Single Market but inside the Schengen travel zone, found it necessary to reach a bilateral agreement with the EU in 2002 to accept the free movement of workers, in exchange for travel and work rights for its own citizens – although Swiss voters narrowly called for quotas of migrants to be restored in a referendum in February 2014. To the academic evidence that immigrants boost the country's economy because they tend to be younger and more industrious than the native population, UKIP also has an answer. In a BBC interview in January 2014, Nigel Farage explained his party's policy of a five-year ban on permanent settlement combined with work permits to meet skills shortages:

If you said to me, 'Would you want to see over the next ten years a further five million people come into Britain and if that happened we would all be slightly richer?', I would say, 'Actually, do you know what? I would rather we weren't slightly richer and I would rather we had communities that felt more united and I would rather have a situation where young unemployed British people had a realistic chance of getting a job.' So, yes, I do think the social side of this matters more than pure market economics.

He would seem to be in tune with voters, with an opinion poll for the BBC by NatCen Social Research finding that 77 per cent wanted fewer immigrants and 56 per cent wanted the number to be 'a lot' lower. Of those who saw immigration as good for the economy, 54 per cent said that they still wanted lower numbers of new arrivals. The question is, how much economic pain is palatable in order to assert tighter control over Britain's borders? With the coalition government aiming to cut annual net migration to below 100,000 a year by 2015 – from 212,000 in the year to September 2013 – even its own Office for Budget Responsibility has used a net figure of 140,000 a year for its forecasts, warning that, with fewer workers coming from abroad, the national debt would be much higher (and by implication so would the need for higher tax or the pressure to cut spending). Restrictions on the rights of European immigrants will play a key part in the renegotiation of Britain's relationship with Brussels planned by David Cameron but, whatever deal he manages, he cannot trump UKIP's promise to take back full control by simply walking away from the EU.

INVESTMENT

IN The UK is the EU's top destination for Foreign Direct Investment (FDI), winning one in five projects in 2012 and a larger market share than in 2011, as well as the highest amounts from the US and Japan.[15] Britain acts as a gateway for investors to the Single Market of 504 million people.

OUT Britain has a range of attractions to persuade international firms to invest such as its flexible and well-educated labour force, quality of life and language advantages, good technology and transport infrastructure, stable and proven domestic legal and political framework, and comparatively low company taxes.

KEY STATS Britain attracted $62 billion in foreign investment in 2012, the highest in Europe and sixth in the world, according to the UN World Investment Report.[16] The UK won 1,559 major investment projects in 2012–13, up 11 per cent after three years of decline, according to UK Trade & Investment.[17] Around half of FDI comes from other EU countries. The UK-based car industry received at least £2.6 billion of foreign investment in 2013.[18]

Nearly 10,000 new cars roll off the Nissan production line in Sunderland every week. Even before it announced an extra £250 million investment to produce its latest top-end Infiniti model from 2015, the company's plant in the north east had already been the biggest car manufacturer in the UK for fifteen consecutive years. Nissan's total investment of £3.5 billion has directly created 6,500 British jobs and a further 23,000 in supply chains. Its success and expansion has encouraged

French components maker Valeo, American car seat supplier Tacle and Japanese exhaust and dashboard maker Calsonic Kansei to come to Britain and set up their own factories. Four out of five of the cars made in Sunderland are exported, with 56 per cent of the 510,572 vehicles made in 2012 going to Europe, 19 per cent staying in the UK, 15 per cent going to Russia and 10 per cent delivered further afield. While the decline of manufacturing is frequently lamented in Britain, the recovery of mass car production, albeit under foreign ownership, has been an outstanding success story in recent years. Foreign Direct Investment (FDI) has revived the (German-owned) Mini as well as (German-owned) Bentley, (Indian-owned) Jaguar Land Rover and (German-owned) Rolls-Royce. The vehicle industry now accounts for 10 per cent of UK exports worth more than £30 billion a year. So it was an important moment when Carlos Ghosn, the chief executive of Nissan, joined the debate about Britain's future with the EU. 'If anything has to change we [would] need to reconsider our strategy and our investments for the future,' he told the BBC at the launch of the firm's Qashqai model in 2012. 'It is a completely different situation if the UK is not part of Europe.' The following year he told an interviewer: 'From the foreign investor point of view I hope that the UK will remain as an EU member.' Ghosn's warnings went to the heart of fears that an exit from the EU would wreck investment in what remains of Britain's manufacturing industry, especially a sector like cars which is so dependent on export sales and component imports.

Eurosceptics were quick to point out that Ghosn had cried wolf before. 'A decade ago, it was not only Nissan but Ghosn himself making remarkably similar imprecise warnings which served to muddy the waters of debate about Europe,' said Global Vision, a eurosceptic campaign group for a basic trade-based relationship with the EU.

Without actually threatening to close the company's Sunderland plant, Ghosn in 2002 warned a UK decision not to join the euro 'might' lead to a reassessment of where to build the next generation of Almera cars. In the end, Britain didn't join the euro and the new Almera was still produced in Sunderland, along with a number of other Nissan models. More than ten years later, business is booming at the plant. Shortly before David Cameron's long-anticipated landmark speech on Europe, Nissan announced a £250 million investment into its UK production facility alongside the creation of 280 new jobs. So should we really be worrying that the ambivalent musings of a company and its boss about our political future with the EU will see them pull the plug on UK production?

But Ghosn was not alone among car-makers in warning about the dangers of withdrawing from the EU. Dave Hodgetts, UK managing director of another Japanese firm, Honda, which has invested at least £1.4 billion in its Swindon plant, said: 'We have very strong markets in Europe, and globally as well, but we are more dependent

on the European region for the exporting of our products. Anything that weakens our ability to trade with
the region would be detrimental to UK manufacturing.'
Stephen Odell, chief executive of Ford in Europe, said:
'All countries should have their sovereignty, but don't
discuss leaving a trading partner where 50 per cent of
your exports go. That would be devastating for the UK
economy.' And Ian Robertson, a BMW board member
and global head of sales, said: 'The UK not only has to
be part of Europe. It has to be a fundamentally active
part of Europe. The thought of a UK outside of Europe
with different trade agreements – sorry, it's not the
way forward.'

While the car-makers made their concerns very clear,
the departure of Britain from the EU would not mean
an automatic crash in automobile production. As Dave
Hodgetts of Honda said: 'It depends on what's negotiated. There would have to be a penalty to being outside
rather than inside – that's the risk I think.' The car
companies are pleading for the stability of the status
quo in dealing with the EU. Will there be penalties for
ending EU membership that would wreck the car industry and dissuade further investment? Campaigners for
withdrawal argue that there need not be any detrimental
impact of Brexit on the success of UK-based car manufacturers. They believe that free trade in goods would
continue between Britain and the twenty-seven remaining EU member states because of a mutual desire to
avoid huge losses on both sides (discussed more fully
in the Trade chapter). To illustrate the folly of failing

to agree a Free Trade Agreement (FTA) on merchandise between an independent Britain and the EU, the eurosceptic Ian Milne, in his paper on The British Car Market and Industry for the Civitas think tank, imagined a telephone call from the German Chancellor to the CEO of BMW.

> Good morning Herr Reithofer. I have some bad news for you, and for your employees. Now that the UK is outside the EU, and there's no UK-EU FTA in place, despite the British offer to scrap duties altogether, the EU and therefore Germany will charge 10 per cent customs duty on car imports from the UK, and the UK will charge 10 per cent customs duty on UK car imports from the EU and therefore from Germany. So, from tomorrow, all of your exports from Bavaria to the UK (130,000 high-end BMWs in 2011) will be 10 per cent more expensive, no doubt giving Jaguar cars produced in England quite a lift. Oh, and just to make your day, all those high-margin Minis you produce in Oxford for export to the EU (156,000 in 2011) will also have to bear the 10 per cent EU duty, making them significantly less competitive in Germany, France and elsewhere in the EU. As for your Rolls-Royces, even wealthy EU buyers might jib at paying the upwards of £10,000 extra that the 10 per cent duty will cause. Sorry about the triple whammy, but that's EU politics for you ... Tschüss!

Milne is right that it is very unlikely that the car industry will be hit with tariffs in a trade war following a British departure from the EU, especially given the German surplus of car sales to the UK (Germany exported 474,000 more cars to the UK in 2011 than it imported from Britain). But even a small amount of uncertainty surrounding the smooth continuance of the free trade in goods between Britain and the EU could affect long-term investment decisions.

This nervousness was shown by the official response of the Japanese government to the Government's Review of the Balance of Competences between the UK and the EU in July 2013:

> More than 1,300 Japanese companies have invested in the UK, as part of the Single Market of the EU, and have created 130,000 jobs, more than anywhere else in Europe. This fact demonstrates that the advantage of the UK as a gateway to the European market has attracted Japanese investment. The government of Japan expects the UK to maintain this favourable role.

One of those Japanese companies is Hitachi Rail Europe, which is building a depot in West London and an £82 million factory to make train carriages in Newton Aycliffe in the north east. Alistair Dormer, the chief executive, echoed the Japanese government line that it had chosen Britain to be its 'gateway' to the EU markets. 'Clearly, we would be concerned as a business if there were any trade barriers or any barriers to doing business in Europe,' he said. Investors wanted Britain to have warm and stable relations with Europe, he added. 'Europe is potentially our biggest market and we would not want anything to happen that would create any barriers or damage the relationship.' He backed calls for structural reforms to the EU, but added: 'My personal advice is we should stay in.' Vince Cable, the Business Secretary, said in January 2014 that he was battling to reassure foreign investors who were increasingly worried about a potential British exit from the EU. 'What I say [to businesses] as a government minister is that the risks of us leaving the EU are very, very low ... and I just try to reassure foreign investors,' he said. 'I was surprised that Japanese companies and government – which are normally quite reticent, they don't normally go to the barricades – came out so openly and said "look, we want certainty".' It was not just investors from Japan who were nervous. Juergen Maier, managing director of Siemens UK, the German engineering giant which employs 13,000 in Britain, told a *Sunday Times* debate on business and the EU that leaving Europe would be 'disastrous' for British manufacturers.

> It's tough enough as it is to convince my board in Germany to invest in the UK for manufacturing. I'm in competition with other European countries, I'm in competition with China. If we were not within the EU, Siemens would make it quite difficult for me to continue to invest in those factories.

Businesses crave stability in the countries they invest in, as reflected in the main factors cited by decision-makers in the annual UK Attractiveness Survey by Ernst

& Young, a professional services company. In its 2013 report, it stated:

> The six aspects of the UK that foreign-based companies consider most attractive from an investment location perspective are: its 'quality of life, diversity, cultural aspects and language' with 91 per cent rating this criterion as very attractive or fairly attractive; 'technology and telecommunications infrastructure' (89 per cent); the 'stability and transparency of the political, legal and regulatory environment' (84 per cent); the 'entrepreneurial culture and entrepreneurship' (also 84 per cent); the 'stability of the social climate' (83 per cent); and 'education in trade and academic disciplines' (80 per cent).

There was no specific question on EU membership as a factor in the decision to come to Britain, although presumably this was part of the 'political, legal and regulatory environment' where stability was viewed as important. However, when Ernst & Young asked investors from around the world what they thought about the prospect of the UK loosening ties with the EU, they found that this was of far more concern to the Europeans than to American or Asian businesses.

> Many commentators in politics and media say that if the UK were to renegotiate its relationship with the European Union to be less integrated than it is today, this would have a damaging effect on foreign direct investment from all parts of the world. This is not necessarily

the case. The picture that emerges from our research is that European companies regard the UK's integration into the EU as being important to the country's attractiveness for FDI, while those in the US and Asia do not.

When existing and potential UK investors were asked whether a lower degree of integration into the EU would make the UK a more attractive place to invest, 72 per cent of companies interviewed in North America and 66 per cent in Asia thought reduced integration would make the UK more attractive for investment, compared to just 38 per cent in Europe.

Our Asian study also shows that a minority of Asian companies – only 48 per cent – find the UK attractive in terms of labour costs. So it appears that companies based in Asian countries may feel that labour costs in the UK could become more attractive if the UK were less subject to EU labour regulation.

The company's 2013 report also warned that Germany was threatening Britain's position as the country of choice for foreign investment, with the highest number of new projects – as opposed to extra investment into existing schemes – going to Germany in 2012. Germany attracts more direct investment from China than the UK. For pro-EU campaigners, the success of Germany in attracting investment, in exporting and in manufacturing is proof that EU membership is no handicap to success in these fields. 'There's a German question for the eurosceptics.

Why is China choosing a country that is locked into the heart of what they see as a moribund union?' wrote the europhile former *Financial Times* editor Richard Lambert in 2013. 'Ten years ago, the UK secured more than three times as many new inward investment projects as Germany. Now, global investors rank us behind Germany as Europe's most attractive country for new investment in the years ahead.' The answer, provided by Ernst & Young, is that Germany excels in sectors in especial demand in the developing world, such as manufacturing, engineering and chemicals. 'Our European survey data suggests that many investors view the UK as being in a different market from Germany for foreign investment, as a result of the two countries' differing economic and market characteristics,' its report concluded.

The UK maintained its lead in the fast-growing business services sector in 2012, as well as in software and financial services, although project numbers in the latter two sectors declined in the year... By contrast, the UK continued to struggle to attract manufacturing, electronics and chemicals foreign direct investment, three sectors that are seen as having real growth potential as the world economy adjusts to rising costs in some previously low-cost destinations. The UK must now identify the sectors in which it can develop a meaningful competitive advantage in attracting investment.

The UK is primarily seen as Europe's leader in the provision of services rather than traditional manufacturing, raw materials or chemicals. As discussed further in the chapters on Trade and also The City and Finance, this makes Britain vulnerable to a failure to negotiate continued full access for its services to the Single Market if it votes to leave the EU, a problem faced by non-EU member Switzerland. For the time being, Mark Gregory, the Ernst & Young chief economist, speaking several months after David Cameron's Bloomberg speech in 2013, said that international companies did not seem too concerned about the possibility of a British referendum on EU membership. He added that they generally believed that, whatever happened in a vote, Britain and the EU would reach a pragmatic arrangement in terms of trade. Jaguar Land Rover's launch of a new £500 million engine plant in Wolverhampton in February 2014 with a promise to employ 1,400 workers suggested that the company's Indian owners had few qualms. Steve Varley, the UK chairman of Ernst & Young, said in 2013 he was confident that Britain would remain Europe's leading destination for foreign investment, partly because of government cuts in corporation tax, adding that he knew of forty multinational companies that were looking at relocating their global or regional headquarters to Britain despite the prospect of an in/out EU referendum. UK corporation tax is set to reduce to 20 per cent in 2015 (it was 30 per cent in 2008), making it the lowest in the G7 group of wealthiest developed nations, compared to the German rate of 29.55 per cent and France's 33.33 per cent. This will go a long way to smoothing over concerns at a fluctuating exchange rate, one of the drawbacks for the UK internationally of not joining the euro, as well as providing a useful hard cash counterweight to less tangible fears about the future outside of the EU.

Almost half of investors surveyed for the government's trade body UK Trade & Investment in 2010 said that a factor in their decision to plough money into the British economy was the ability to serve the European market from a base in an English-speaking country. But it was not given as the most important factor in their decision, with 90 per cent of respondents saying that their top motivation was servicing the UK market. Being close to customers and being able to access centres of expertise were also among the reasons given. The Business, Innovation and Skills Department has concluded that 'surveys suggest that access to the Single Market is not the sole reason for choosing the UK as a destination for investment. Being a global hub, having a good established business network, the English language and good international linkages were all cited as factors.' A House of Commons Library report in September 2013 on the Economic Impact of EU Membership on the UK concluded:

On the whole, it is reasonable to conclude that membership of the Single Market is one of a number of important determinants of FDI... On the one hand, the removal of barriers to trade eliminates an important incentive to physically locate abroad, meaning the Single Market could be argued to discourage intra-EU investment. On the other, membership of the Single Market should stimulate inward investment in the UK from outside the EU, since by doing so, they can access twenty-seven other EU markets tariff-free.

Maintaining this tariff-free access to the rest of the EU was the fundamental reason for the appeals from UK-based car companies, Hitachi Rail and the Japanese government itself to keep the status quo in trade relations with the EU from the perspective of international investors. Back in 2000, research on the jobs linked to EU membership by the National Institute for Economic and Social Research (NIESR) warned that a breakdown in trade relations could mean a drop of one third in foreign investment in manufacturing and one tenth in services. The challenge for British negotiators in the event of Brexit – if they want to preserve current high levels of foreign investment – is to keep the open border trading relationship with European neighbours. Otherwise there could be a sizeable reduction in foreign firms willing to put money into the British economy, and that would worsen living standards. As Simon Tilford at the Centre for European Reform argued:

Foreign owners, foreign capital is more mobile than domestic capital, so if Britain withdraws from the EU and foreign owners of assets in the UK consider that move a threat to their business ... they are much more likely to reduce investment or repatriate their businesses than are domestically owned businesses which are more susceptible to political pressure to remain in the country.

Brexit could still bring some benefits for investors, the House of Commons report added.

Outside the EU, the UK may be able to establish a regulatory regime more favourable to overseas investors that could offset the effect of its departure. In particular, the UK would regain competence to negotiate international agreements on Foreign Direct Investment with other countries, something which it has not been able to do since the Lisbon Treaty entered force in 2009.

JOBS

IN Pro-EU politicians regularly argue that at least 3 million jobs depend on Britain's EU membership, implying that these would be at risk if the UK left.

OUT If Britain does a deal to remain in the EU's Single Market, like non-EU member Norway, or negotiates a Free Trade Agreement to retain full trading access, then many of the supposed job losses will be avoided. Jobs lost by leaving the EU would eventually be replaced as trade expands elsewhere.

KEY STATS South Bank University in 2000 said that 3.45 million UK jobs were related to trade with the EU; the National Institute of Economic and Social Research in 2000 put the figure at 3.2 million jobs. With 29.4 million employed in the UK in 2012, these reports suggest that more than one in ten jobs are related to the EU.

Business for Britain was created in April 2013 to campaign for a significant return of EU powers under David Cameron's policy of renegotiating the UK's relationship before holding a referendum on membership. To add weight to its goal of a dramatically slimmed-down deal with Brussels, the eurosceptic organisation commissioned extensive polling that showed businesses believed the costs of the Single Market outweighed the benefits. Not mentioned in a 26-page report issued by Business for Britain on its polling results, however, was another finding that showed 6 per cent of firms (sixty-two out of 1,024) surveyed said they would be forced to close down in the UK if voters decided to leave the EU. Based on turnover, half of these were small businesses, 32 per cent medium-sized and 18 per cent large. The overlooked finding was discovered in the small print of the research and highlighted by British Influence, another group created in response to Cameron's referendum plan. British Influence is a pro-European group formed to campaign for the positive engagement of the UK in the EU. It quickly realised that talk of business closures and therefore job losses could help its argument for staying in the EU and its Single Market. It scaled up the forecasts based on 1,024 responses to all businesses in the UK and concluded that 1.5 million jobs were at risk. 'Tucked away amidst all these interesting results is a bombshell,' wrote Peter Wilding of British Influence on the ConservativeHome website in November 2013.

On page sixteen of the poll is the conclusion that over 50,000 businesses would close if the UK left Europe – putting 1.5 million jobs at high-risk. Those 5 per cent of small businesses, 8 per cent of medium-sized ones and 9 per cent of large ones, which said they would close, equates to 1,501,040 jobs – according to figures worked out by British Influence with the help of a professional statistician. The Department for Business, Innovation and Skills works this out at around 50,000 small, 2,500 medium and 500 large companies at risk of closure. Worse still, these figures for business closures and job losses could also more than double, since 7 per cent of all businesses surveyed would be 'unsure' about their future if Britain left the EU after a referendum.

Not only was this a taste of the arguments to come if and when the EU referendum is called, but it was also the first time in nearly thirteen years that a clear figure had been put on direct job losses from Brexit. Before this, politicians continued to use figures from 2000, when two pieces of academic research concluded that either 3.45 million or 3.2 million UK jobs were related to trade with the EU. The 1.5 million estimate was less than half of this amount but the first based on extensive polling data. It was also more concretely related to jobs that would actually be lost in the event of British departure. As Peter Wilding pointed out: 'People we are supposed to support are saying: if we leave, we will close and jobs will go.'

It was about time that the figure of more than 3 million potential job losses was laid to rest. No politician has been more fond of repeating the claim than Nick Clegg, who uses it to suggest that leaving the EU will jeopardise that number of jobs. As recently as August 2013, Clegg told the *Newcastle Journal* that

there are up to 3.5 million jobs either directly or indirectly linked to our membership of the world's biggest single market, and yet, because of political dogma, UKIP and the Conservatives want to put that at risk. Yes, the EU needs to reform, but people should remember this is about people's jobs, their monthly pay packet, and they shouldn't play around with that.

The pro-EU Labour MP Keith Vaz has also used the figure, telling the *Sunday Mirror* in January 2013 that 'over half of trade and 3.5 million jobs in Britain are dependent on the EU'. Gordon Brown challenged the then opposition leader David Cameron at Prime Minister's Question Time in 2008, saying, 'Why won't you wake up to the fact that 3.5 million jobs are dependent on our membership of the EU?' But even the authors of the original studies do not believe that 3.5 million jobs will be lost if Britain were to leave the EU.

The figure originates from two pieces of research commissioned in 2000 by another, long defunct, pressure group called Britain in Europe, which campaigned for Britain to join the euro. In one study, the European Institute at South Bank University said that exports to the EU generated direct employment of 2.53 million jobs in British industry and supply chains, while the secondary impact of spending on British goods and services arising from revenue generated by exporting to the EU supported 'indirect employment effects' amounting to a further 917,000 jobs. The report said that:

> The aim of the present investigation is not an overall evaluation of EU membership, but rather an estimate of the employment effects that result from the exports of goods and services from the UK to the EU. Although many previous studies have sought to answer the question of what would have happened if Britain were not a member of the EU, we do not seek to test this counterfactual hypothesis.

The researchers used export figures from 1997, when trade with the EU (then fourteen member states) made up 55.8 per cent of British goods exports (it had fallen to 50.3 per cent in 2013 for twenty-six member states[19]) and 34.4 per cent of British services exports (it was 35.2 per cent in 2012[20]). A key variable in the researchers' calculations (the import component of exports) was taken from 1990, which was the best available figure at the time. The data is now long out of date.

The second study was by the National Institute for Economic and Social Research (NIESR) in London which calculated that about 2.7 million British jobs were directly related to goods and services sold to the EU, while a further 500,000 were supported by other sources of demand for firms which derive much of their activity from exporting to Europe. That made 3.2 million jobs linked to trade with the EU. The report added:

> As the experience of the 1960s indicates, there is no reason why being outside the EU should necessarily involve mass unemployment, although living standards would probably be slightly lower ... exports to the rest of the EU would not fall to zero if the UK were to leave the EU.

The report concluded that living standards would be affected by EU withdrawal, with gross national income declining after twenty years by 1.5 per cent and output by 2 per cent. As mentioned in the previous chapter, it warned that Foreign Direct Investment in manufacturing in Britain could drop by a third and in services by 10 per cent if Britain pulled out of the EU. As for job losses in the event of British withdrawal from Brussels, around 175,000 would be lost after three years, but these would be reabsorbed at lower wage levels in the longer term, the report estimated. 'There is no *a priori* reason to suppose that many of these [jobs], if any, would be lost permanently if Britain were to leave the EU,' it concluded. So, according to research commissioned in 2000 by the pro-euro Britain in Europe, there would be similar levels of jobs whether the UK was in or out of the EU, although they would probably be paid at a slightly lower level. In a statement at the time, as the figures began to be used as a political football, Martin Weale, then director of the NIESR, said: 'Although a large number of jobs are now connected to EU exports and the income they generate, it is not the case that many of these would be lost permanently if Britain was to leave the EU.' One of the authors of the South Bank research, Professor Iain Begg, said in 2011 that he would not expect mass redundancies if Britain withdrew from the EU, on the assumption that there would be some kind of deal to continue with trade, even if the UK was no longer involved in setting the rules in Brussels. And Jonathan Portes, the current director of the NIESR, tweeted in September 2013 that the research was 'past [its] sell-by date'. In an article, he called the claim that up to three million jobs would be jeopardised by a British departure one of the great red herrings of the EU debate.

Even if the potential negative impact on trade and invest-ment ... were actually to materialise, such claims are totally implausible, and certainly not based on evidence. Over the medium to long run, the main determinant of employment and unemployment is the supply side of the economy – the flexibility of the labour market and the skills and qualifications of potential workers – so there is unlikely to be any significant long-run impact. Trade makes us richer and more productive – so a reduction in trade may well feed through to a reduction in real wages – but most conventional economic models do not suggest that it creates (or destroys) substantial numbers of jobs over the medium term.

Full Fact, the independent fact-checking organisation, has twice issued warnings to politicians about their continued use of the 'more than three million jobs' scare over EU withdrawal. In its first review in November 2011, it said that

any statistics based purely on trade with the EU do not offer a fair cost-benefit analysis of the impact of EU membership on the labour market, since the two are not necessarily directly correlated. Free trade agreements between the EU and non-EU countries exist for some ten countries in Europe and others elsewhere, including a Free Trade Agreement made with Switzerland in 1972. A figure which depends entirely on UK exports with the EU does not necessarily show that UK withdrawal from the EU would dramatically alter this trade in a negative way.

In its second review in July 2013, it added:

The point is that the three million figure doesn't tell us anything about the number of jobs linked to British membership of the EU as an institution, only about those linked to the EU as an export market. What would happen to that market in the event of a British exit is a matter of speculation. This is no small distinction to make and, with a referendum in the horizon, it's only fair that the public are supplied with the correct information to inform their vote. Unfortunately certain politicians have made a habit of conflating the two, with Danny Alexander [the Liberal Democrat Chief Secretary to the Treasury] following in the footsteps of Nick Clegg and Ed Balls [Labour's shadow Chancellor] on this matter. We are concerned this number has acquired a life of its own and are therefore writing to those concerned to ask that greater care is used in the future to avoid misunderstanding about this figure.

That leaves the figure of 1.5 million job losses based on Business for Britain polling in 2013 and extrapolated by British Influence. This is a warning of how bad things could get if there is a catastrophic breakdown of trading relations between the EU and Britain after a vote to leave. It would not necessarily apply if the UK were able to stay in the Single Market like Norway or negotiate a Free Trade Agreement to have full access for those companies that continued to meet EU standards and rules even though Britain has withdrawn from political involvement. As discussed in the previous chapter over the car industry, there is every incentive for Germany in particular and the EU in general to continue to keep close trading links with Britain in the event of its withdrawal from the EU. Around one million jobs in Germany, 500,000 jobs in France and 300,000 jobs in Italy are said to be linked to exporting to the UK. Some eurosceptics claim that Brexit will bring a domestic jobs boom. The Bruges Group, a think tank opposed to European integration, has argued that a million jobs would be created in Britain by leaving the EU but staying in the European Economic Area, like Norway, because of the effective tax cut for businesses freed from 70 per cent of the EU's rules and regulations.[21] As discussed in other chapters, particularly on the City and Investment, some sectors will go through a turbulent readjustment period and probably see jobs lost in the UK if the relationship with the EU changes. But the level of job losses depends on a 'known unknown' – the exact status of the new relationship between Brussels and the UK. If a post-Brexit Britain can only achieve the same level of access as Switzerland, which has free trade in goods but not completely in services, the financial sector is likely to see thousands of jobs disappear as international banks, finance and insurance companies move staff into the EU. There are also areas where new jobs could be created, including opportunities arising from trade deals between Britain and other countries which are not possible while the EU retains full control of international trading policy, and job-creating freedoms for smaller companies released from European social and employment regulations.

PEACE AND HUMAN RIGHTS

IN The European Union was awarded the 2012 Nobel Peace Prize for advancing the causes of peace, reconciliation, democracy and human rights in Europe. The EU has provided the political and economic framework for peace among nations that went to war with each other regularly for centuries and bound together France and Germany which fought three times in seventy years.

OUT Britain would continue to be a key member of NATO which is also responsible for binding European nations together and guaranteeing the peace since the Second World War. Would the UK's departure really fuel a rise in separatism and hostility that eventually results in the disintegration of the EU and war?

KEY STATS More than 50 million lives were lost in the Second World War, making it the deadliest conflict in history, which started just two decades after the First World War claimed more than 10 million lives.

Edward Heath, the man who took Britain into the European Economic Community in 1973, was named after his uncle – a man he never knew because he was among the one million Britons killed in the Great War of 1914–18. As a 21-year-old undergraduate, the future Conservative Prime Minister went on a student exchange trip to Germany in 1937 to see for himself the Nazi regime that came to power in the years of economic depression and would soon plunge Europe into an even more devastating conflict. Heath was introduced to two of the senior Nazis, Joseph Goebbels and Heinrich Himmler, and watched in horror as Adolf Hitler gave one of his trademark ranting speeches at a Nuremberg rally. The following year Heath experienced conflict in Europe for the first time when he came under machine-gun fire on a visit to Spain to meet leaders of the Popular Front resisting General Franco's forces. Just a few years later, as a captain in the Royal Artillery, Heath joined the Normandy landings and the Allied advance across war-ravaged Europe, taking part in the destruction of the French cathedral city of Caen and being greeted by cheering crowds in liberated Antwerp. He saw at first hand the ruins of German cities like Düsseldorf which were unrecognisable as the places he had visited just a few years earlier. 'The centre was nothing but a mass of rubble. It proved impossible for me to find my way to the street, let alone the house, where I had stayed as a student,' he wrote. Promoted to the rank of major, Heath's unit was put in charge of a prisoner-of-war camp near Hannover and Heath even commanded a firing squad that executed a Polish prisoner for rape. 'My generation could not live in the past,' Heath wrote about his ambition to see Europe united in peace. 'We had to work for the future. We were surrounded by destruction, homelessness, hunger and despair. Only by working together had we any hope of creating a society which would uphold the true values of European civili-sation.' The EEC, the forerunner of the European Union, was created by men like Heath who had experienced the horrors of two wars initiated by European enemies.

David Cameron declined to attend the Nobel Peace Prize ceremony for the EU in Oslo in December 2012 but paid tribute in his Bloomberg speech to the part played by the European Union in maintaining peace between the continental powers. He acknowledged that today's generation accepted almost unthinkingly that peace was the permanent state of international relations in Europe. 'What Churchill described as the twin marauders of war and tyranny have been almost entirely banished from our continent,' he said.

> Today, hundreds of millions dwell in freedom, from the Baltic to the Adriatic, from the Western Approaches to the Aegean. And while we must never take this for granted, the first purpose of the European Union – to secure peace – has been achieved and we should pay tribute to all those in the EU, alongside NATO, who made that happen. But today the main, over-riding purpose of the European Union is different: not to win peace, but to secure prosperity.

It could be argued that the two fundamental goals, peace and prosperity, go hand in hand, given the role played by the economic crisis of the 1930s in the rise of Nazism. A similar sense of national crisis and exploitation by foreign powers has been felt during the six-year recession in Greece and spawned a menacing far-right movement, Golden Dawn, even as the EU was awarded the Nobel Prize for contributing to 'the advancement of peace and reconciliation, democracy and human rights in Europe'. The award also conveniently overlooked the murderous conflict in the Balkans in the 1990s following the break-up of Yugoslavia when more than 100,000 lost their lives and which the EU was powerless to prevent despite its attempts at diplomacy. In presenting the prize, the official announcement did acknowledge that 'the EU is currently undergoing grave economic difficulties and considerable social unrest' but added that

> the Norwegian Nobel Committee wishes to focus on what it sees as the EU's most important result: the successful struggle for peace and reconciliation and for democracy and human rights. The stabilising part played by the EU has helped to transform most of Europe from a continent of war to a continent of peace.

Although the Nobel award specifically mentioned the EU's work for human rights, it is important to be clear that the EU is a separate organisation to the Council of Europe – the body which oversees the European Court of Human Rights. Popular confusion between the two is understandable. A pan-European human rights body was a brainchild of Winston Churchill, Britain's wartime Prime Minister, at the same time as he also called for a political alliance of European nations. 'We must recreate the European family in a regional structure called, it may be, the United States of Europe,' he said in a landmark speech in Zurich in 1946. 'The first step is to form a Council of Europe.' (Although Churchill was not always clear about Britain's role as an observer or a participant in these European organisations, he also said in Zurich that 'in all this urgent work, France and Germany must take the lead together. Great Britain, the British Commonwealth of Nations, mighty America, and I trust Soviet Russia – for then indeed all would be well – must be the friends and sponsors of the new Europe and must champion its right to live and shine.') Churchill took part in the first sessions of the Council of Europe assembly in 1949 and 1950 when British lawyers helped to draft the European Convention on Human Rights, which was designed to protect citizens from a return to the barbarity of Nazism or the oppression of Communism by guaranteeing – among other things – rights to life, liberty, freedom of expression and a fair trial. All member states of the Council of Europe agree to abide by the Convention and accept judgments on it by the European Court of Human Rights (ECHR) set up in 1959. Although its judgments are binding on member nations, it has no means of enforcement other than moral authority.

The British government complained that the ECHR exceeded its mandate to stand up for the oppressed when it ruled that denying prisoners in Britain the right to vote breached their human rights, as did passing 'whole life' sentences with no chance of review. So, as the Conservative Party was squaring up to the EU with plans for a renegotiation of powers and a referendum on membership, it was also clashing with the Council of Europe over these two ECHR rulings, as well as judgments which held up the extradition of radical Islamists

Abu Hamza to the US and Abu Qatada to Jordan. 'If Parliament decides that prisoners should not get the vote then I think they damn well shouldn't. It should be a national decision taken by our Parliament,' David Cameron said in December 2013. Cameron vowed to restrict the court's powers, saying 'we need to clip its wings'. However, the ECHR's real power over British law comes from British legislation, the Human Rights Act 1998, which gave the Convention legal force in British courts. That is why the Conservatives plan to repeal the Act, although Theresa May went further, telling the 2013 Conservative party conference that 'the next Conservative manifesto will promise to scrap the Human Rights Act ... [and] if leaving the European Convention is what it takes to fix our human rights law, that is what we should do'. Thorbjørn Jagland, secretary-general of the Council of Europe, warned against the UK as a founder member of the human rights system refusing to enforce ECHR judgments. 'If we start to pick and choose the judgments from the court, then the court will be weakened and have no meaning,' Jagland said. 'Europe cannot afford to let the UK leave the whole convention system which is so important from a pan-European perspective ... the UK is the best pupil in the class. It has always been seen as the leading nation on human rights.' The concern is that without Britain on board, there will be little chance of ECHR rulings being followed in less savoury corners of Europe.

The British debate over the ECHR comes, confusingly, in parallel with the EU deepening its own human rights powers. In recent years the EU has sought to become more of a 'rights body' not only for its own member states and their neighbours but for the globe. In 2007, the EU set up a Fundamental Rights Agency based in Vienna to monitor racism and xenophobia; it also set up an EU Institute for Gender Equality based in Vilnius. In 2012, José Manuel Barroso said: 'We need to reinforce our Common Foreign and Security Policy and a common approach to defence matters because together we have the power and the scale to shape the world into a fairer, rules-based and human rights abiding place.' The original EEC treaty did not have any reference to human rights but the European Court of Justice first claimed jurisdiction over fundamental rights in 1970. The EU seriously began to encroach upon the role of the Council of Europe in 2000 when it adopted a Charter of Fundamental Rights containing fifty-four rights (the original Convention had eighteen Articles) including the right to strike, to marry and found a family, to collective bargaining and fair working conditions. It was incorporated into EU law in the Lisbon Treaty of 2009, although Britain and Poland secured a protocol to exempt their legal systems from any new rights. In 2013, however, the legal effectiveness of the protocol was called into question, when High Court judge Justice Mostyn called it a 'misleading product of political compromise because on any view the charter enunciated a host of new rights not expressly found in the European Convention on Human Rights'.

Could these rights be applied in the UK? Rosalind English, editor of the UK Human Rights blog, said that

the EU's European Court of Justice argued that the UK
was not exempt from obligations to comply. If that was
right, she said that the charter introduced into domestic
law all those parts of the ECHR that were deliberately
missed out by Parliament when passing the Human
Rights Act 1998, plus 'a great deal more', including social
and economic rights. In Mostyn's view 'it would seem
that the much wider charter of rights is now part of our
domestic law' and would remain so, even if the Human
Rights Act was repealed. This led Lord Mance, a justice
of the UK Supreme Court, to warn that the European
Court of Justice was attempting to impose the Charter
of Fundamental Rights on British judges. 'Ultimately, the
European project must rest on mutual trust, goodwill and
cooperation,' he said in a speech to a legal conference in
2013. 'Mutual trust is an article of faith of the European
Union. But it requires real sensitivity to build and maintain. Over-ambitious steam-rolling of centralising projects
in order to promote the European project can achieve
precisely the opposite result.' The Fresh Start group of
Conservative MPs campaigning to reduce the EU's powers
warned that a treaty change – agreed unanimously by the
twenty-eight member states – was needed for a secure
British opt-out from the Charter of Fundamental Rights.
'The UK should now seek further changes to the EU treaties in order to cement an opt-out from the Charter,' the
group said in its Mandate for Reform of November 2013.

The development of the EU into a global peace-
promoting rights body is being led by the European
External Action Service (EEAS) created in the Lisbon

Treaty to represent the EU around the world. Under its first head, the Labour peer Baroness Ashton of Upholland, the EEAS created the new post of EU Special Representative (EUSR) for Human Rights. Stavros Lambrinidis, a former MEP and Foreign Minister of Greece, was chosen to travel the world pressing the case for the downtrodden and campaigning against the death penalty. 'All trade and cooperation agreements with third countries contain a clause stipulating that human rights are an essential element in relations between the parties,' the EEAS says on its website.

The Union's human rights policy encompasses civil, political, economic, social and cultural rights. It also seeks to promote the rights of women, of children, of those persons belonging to minorities, and of displaced persons. With a budget of €1.1 billion between 2007 and 2013, the European Instrument for Democracy and Human Rights supports non-governmental organisations. In particular it supports those promoting human rights, democracy and the rule of law; abolishing the death penalty; combating torture; and fighting racism and other forms of discrimination.

The European Parliament also keeps up the pressure for advancing human rights, including gender equality. Mary Honeyball, a Labour MEP, said:

Equal pay for equal work was enshrined as one of the core principles of the EU in its 1957 founding treaty –

thirteen years before it was introduced in the UK – and since then Europe has consistently led from the front. The aim of the current parliament is 'inclusive growth': last year we resolved to achieve 40 per cent representation for women on company boards by 2020, and to, by the same point, eliminate the gender pay gap across Europe. These two resolutions were the inspiration for Gender 2020, my effort to keep the debate going and ensure we in Britain do our bit to achieve this. At present we have the sixth widest gender pay gap in Europe, and only the tenth highest proportion of women on boards (a pretty unimpressive state of affairs, given we're Europe's financial capital). Like my colleagues on the Women's Rights committee, I want to see gender equality from the tip to the base of the jobs pyramid by 2020. I want this to exist across Europe – and I want Britain to be among the first countries to deliver it.

A British withdrawal from the EU would not stop its self-declared mission to spread peace and human rights. In some areas it would lead to a more coherent EU that no longer had to deal with British resistance to closer harmonisation of defence, employment and social affairs, foreign policy, justice and home affairs, migration policy, tax and economic matters to name just the most prominent areas of regular disagreement. But could a British departure have the ultimate effect of tearing apart the EU itself and – as the first serious backwards step since the Treaty of Rome was signed by the first six member states in 1957 – be the beginning of the end of the dream of a united Europe? Some commentators foresee other nations emboldened to quit the EU by a British withdrawal. 'There would be many unintended consequences from a Brexit, of course, depending on how skilfully Britain's exit treaty was drafted,' wrote Hugo Brady of the Centre for European Reform in November 2013.

> If one Union member secedes, that increases the chances of another many times over: Denmark and the Czech Republic might look to the door ... as could, let's say, a newly arrived member state defying Brussels over the rule of law and human rights. So the other members and the institutions are unlikely to make Britain's exit treaty favourable for their own individual reasons and to protect the integrity of the Union. But it is still quite likely that if Britain left, other countries would eventually too.

The enormous sums of money handed to poorer countries to invest in their infrastructure would certainly make newer member states think hard before leaving, making the richer, northern nations the most likely candidates to follow an independent Britain out of the EU. But the loss of Denmark or Sweden would not be terminal to the EU. The organisation fundamentally exists to bind together France and Germany, the two countries at the heart of the terrible conflicts that caused so much destruction in the past two centuries, from Napoleon to Hitler. Although there can be no doubting the sense of crisis if a founder member like the Netherlands quit, only a French or German departure would destroy the EU and threaten the European peace we take for granted. And after Jacques Chirac followed Tony Blair in calling a referendum on the EU Constitution in 2005 only to see it lost, Paris has learned its lesson on putting the EU to a public vote.

PROSPERITY

IN The Single Market has boosted national income through increased trade between European nations. The overall impact of the EU on prosperity is less clear, however, because of the costs of regulation, customs duty on non-EU imports, higher food prices and the disputed impact of EU migrants.

OUT Britain could try to negotiate full access to the Single Market to maintain strong trading and travel links. It would be free to make its own trade deals with non-EU countries and cut duties on imports. Only if it left the Single Market, however, could it also scrap expensive red tape for businesses and control EU immigration more tightly.

KEY STATS The government says the benefit of the Single Market is worth £3,500 per household. The Confederation of British Industry claims that the EU benefits the UK by £62–78 billion a year. In 2013, deductions and receipts from Britain's gross EU membership fee of £17.18 billion left a net contribution of £8.62 billion (for a full breakdown of Britain's EU contributions, rebate and receipts see table on page 246).

At the dawn of the millennium, the EU set out an ambitious ten-year plan to succeed in the new century. The Lisbon Strategy, signed in the Portuguese capital in March 2000 by the then fifteen member nations under the chairmanship of Prime Minister António Guterres, aimed to 'make Europe by 2010 the most competitive and the most dynamic knowledge-based economy in the world capable of sustainable economic growth with more and better jobs and greater social cohesion'. The plan aimed to see 70 per cent of the adult population in work, up from 63.4 per cent in 2000. The ultimate goal was 'to enable the Union to regain the conditions for full employment'. This was to be achieved by a mixture of the economic competitiveness typical of northern European nations and the social support systems championed by France and other southern countries. There were targets to increase training, cut red tape for new company start-ups and fund millions of euros of research projects. 'The Lisbon Strategy is going to bring about a revolution in the way we work,' said Mr Guterres. Fellow centre-left leader Chancellor Gerhard Schroeder of Germany said that 'it shows we are prepared to move away from the old industrial society toward a new, high-technology and communications-based one'. It was, as the *International Herald Tribune* observed, 'a bid to surpass the United States in the Internet age'. It didn't work. There were to be no European rivals to touch the success of Amazon, eBay, Facebook, Google, Microsoft or Twitter. By 2010, the European economy was in the middle of a double-dip recession and unemployment was steadily rising.

To be fair, the failure of the Lisbon Strategy was not entirely Europe's fault. The economy was hit by the financial hurricane which started in the US with the collapse of Lehman Brothers investment bank. But even before then the EU never looked like meeting its targets, with employment peaking at 67.1 per cent in the fifteen member states in 2008 (the addition of ten eastern European countries in 2004 brought the overall rate down further) and falling to 65.8 per cent by 2010. Portugal itself fared particularly badly, with a recession soon claiming the job of Mr Guterres in 2001 and the euro crisis forcing the country to take drastic reforms that cut the employment rate to 61.8 per cent by 2012. Prosperity was replaced in many EU member states by austerity, with the most devastating effects seen in Greece, where the level of unemployment among those aged under twenty-five reached 60 per cent in January 2013, and Spain, where it hit 56.8 per cent in September 2013.[22] Europe felt more like a continent in decline by the end of the Lisbon Strategy with a level of social payments considered unsupportable by Mr Schroeder's replacement as the German Chancellor, Angela Merkel. 'If Europe today accounts for just over 7 per cent of the world's population, produces around 25 per cent of global GDP and has to finance 50 per cent of global social spending, then it is obvious that it will have to work very hard to maintain its prosperity and way of life,' she said in December 2011.

Outside the straitjacket of the single currency, Britain avoided the worst of the euro crisis. David Cameron maintained in his Bloomberg speech that 'today the main overriding purpose of the European Union is ... to secure prosperity'. But assessing just how important the EU is to the UK's standard of living is notoriously difficult to do and no government has attempted a cost-benefit analysis of membership or even commissioned an independent study. There are various claims about the extra wealth generated by the EU's Single Market, which has undeniably increased trade and commerce between the twenty-eight member states and added to Britain's national income. There are also some negative factors to be taken into account on the balance sheet when working out the overall impact of the EU, however. These include the cost of regulations, higher food prices as a result of the Common Agricultural Policy, missed global opportunities as a result of focusing on the European market, more expensive imports from outside the EU thanks to the tariffs and quotas of its Customs Union, and, of course, Britain's membership fee. The bigger picture of prosperity is further complicated by the economic and social impact of intra-EU migration. Put all these together in one giant calculation and some analysts believe that the purely economic impact of membership is negligible. Others have claimed gains of up to 6 per cent of GDP, although how much of this would be permanently lost in the event of leaving the EU is also hotly debated. With so many variables, the outcome of cost-benefit studies often seem to reflect the author's attitude towards the importance of the EU itself.

The starting point of these calculations is the contribution transferred from the Account of Her Majesty's Exchequer held at the Bank of England to the European Commission in twice monthly instalments. The gross total of £17.18 billion in 2013 was reduced by £3.32 billion thanks to Britain's rebate deal to £13.86 billion, or £38 million a day. The UK received public sector funding of £5.24 billion back from Brussels, leaving a net contribution of £8.62 billion, according to Treasury provisional figures.[23] Around £925 million was also received in the form of grants directly to the private sector, mainly for research, while £327 million was transferred from the UK in overseas aid channelled through the European Development Fund run by the European Commission and additional to the EU budget. The rebate, won by Margaret Thatcher in 1984 after nearly five years of negotiation, has saved £79.7 billion over thirty years. That's £7.3 million a day. In contrast to entire EU spending of €132.9 billion in 2013, the UK government planned to spend £720 billion. 'The European Union's budget is modest in size compared to national wealth,' said José Manuel Barroso, announcing agreement on an EU seven-year framework budget of nearly €1 trillion for 2014–20. While this will be roughly 1 per cent of the EU's Gross National Income, it is misleading to compare it to national spending because the EU is a bureaucracy which does not pay for public sector workers such as nurses, teachers, social workers or an army, even if its laws increasingly affect their working lives. The sum total of EU GNI has also increased greatly as the number of member states expanded from nine when Britain joined to twenty-eight, putting unexpected extra cost burdens on net contributors like the UK. The Account of Her Majesty's Exchequer now pays six times more in real terms to Brussels than it did in 1973.

Britain is consistently the second-largest net funder of EU coffers behind Germany and ahead of Italy and France. Most of the money goes towards subsidising farmers and funding infrastructure and employment projects, especially in poorer regions of Europe. In 2013, the proportion of the EU budget spent on the Common Agricultural Policy was 39 per cent, or €57 billion, way out of kilter with its EU average gross value added contribution to the economy of 1.7 per cent – and just 0.7 per cent in the UK. British farmers and landowners receive funding from Brussels under two main headings, direct farm payments and rural development, but the UK's net contribution to the agriculture budget – sometimes portrayed as a subsidy to competitors – amounted to €3.4 million a day. According to an analysis by the OECD, European taxpayers paid €105 billion in 2008 to farmers through subsidies and tariffs, as well as national programmes. Just over half of this came directly from the EU budget. The UK's share of the total was around €8.27 billion, made up of €4.6 billion in farm subsidies through EU and national spending, while British consumers paid a premium for their food of €3.67 billion.[24] With 25.5 million households in the UK, that worked out at €324 each extra per year for agricultural support. If Britain left the EU, it would escape the Common Agricultural Policy but would almost certainly need to give some funding to its farmers to ensure that they did not lose out to subsidised overseas rivals. It is not just farm products, however, but a range of goods imported from outside the EU that are more expensive because of the EU's common external tariff, such as footwear with a border tax of up to 17 per cent and most other clothing which is charged 12 per cent to enter the EU. Some of these tariffs could be cut by an independent Britain, as they exist to protect jobs in other EU countries, for example shoe production in Italy. 'Although they [tariffs] raise prices for consumers, they also help producers by shielding them from more price competitive imports,' said a research paper on the economic impact of the EU by the House of Commons Library in September 2013. 'While the government would be free to set its own tariffs outside the EU, removing the protection they afford to certain industries could prove politically difficult, given that the costs will be specific and localised, but the benefits diffuse,' it added.

The difficulty of putting a single number on the economic impact of Britain's EU membership over the years was neatly summed up by a House of Commons Library review of the various attempts:

Many of the costs and benefits are, in certain respects, subjective, diffuse or intangible; and partly because a host of assumptions must be made about the terms on which the UK would depart the EU, and how the government would fill the policy vacuum left in areas where the EU currently has competence. Any estimate of the effects of withdrawal will be highly sensitive to such assumptions, and can thus be embedded with varying degrees of optimism. This perhaps helps to explain why the wide range of estimates from the EU cost-benefit 'literature' can appear influenced by the prior convictions of those conducting the analysis.

Even an evaluation of the Single Market requires layers of complicated economic modelling and many 'heroic assumptions' according to one such study by the Centre for Economic Policy Research (CEPR) in 2008, written by academics from Oxford and Berkeley, California. Its ultimate conclusion was that 'European incomes would have been roughly 5 per cent lower today in the absence of the EU'. The creation of the Common Market and its Customs Union brought about a step change in growth, it said, because politicians could appeal to the spirit of European integration to overcome strong domestic resistance to labour market reforms and the liberalisation of protected sectors. The UK 'almost certainly' suffered substantial losses as a result of the Common Agricultural Policy but, if it had never existed, countries 'would probably have gone on protecting their farmers' anyway, they said. The Single Market achieved fewer gains than the original Common Market, the study argued, because 'the 1980s was a period that saw a good deal of domestic liberalisation and deregulation in Europe, spurred by the examples of Reagan in the United States and Thatcher in the United Kingdom'.

A more specific UK analysis by the Institute of Economic Affairs updated in 2001 concluded that:

Many costs and benefits of EU membership are intangible ... An assessment of those costs and benefits which can be quantified suggests the net effect of withdrawal on the British economy would be small – probably less than 1 per cent of GDP. If a special relationship with

the rest of the EU were arranged, there might be a
small benefit.

Leaving the Common Agricultural Policy would represent 'a clear gain to Britain' and, while there might be
a loss in Foreign Direct Investment, 'fear of adverse
economic consequences should not deter a British
government from seeking to change the relationship
of the UK with the EU, or, in the last resort, from leaving
the Union'. According to an Institute of Directors paper
in 2000, 'the costs of EU membership outweigh the benefits significantly. Moreover, because of the significance of
the CAP, there is a huge discrepancy between those who
receive (farmers) and those who give (taxpayers).' The
IoD put the cost impact of the Common Agricultural
Policy as 1 per cent of GDP and the annual cost to the
UK economy of the 'EU social welfare model' at another
1 per cent. Overall, it decided that the net annual cost of
EU membership was 1.75 per cent of GDP.

A report by the generally pro-EU National Institute
of Economic and Social Research (NIESR) in 2000
came to the opposite conclusion, saying that 'the level
of real gross national income would be approximately
1.5 to 1.75 per cent lower outside the EU than inside'
with GDP permanently 2.25 percentage points lower. It
reviewed investment by US-owned companies in Europe
since the mid-1960s and argued 'that membership of
the EU ... and hence participation in the Single Market
Programme [has] a significant positive impact on the
location and scale of investment'. In 2004 the think tank

Civitas claimed that the annual direct net cost of EU membership was probably 4 per cent of GDP, made up of £20 billion from regulation, £15 billion from the CAP and £5 billion from the net membership fee. The study claimed that there was 'an absence of any convincing evidence in the UK or elsewhere that the Single Market has actually delivered net benefits for the economies of member states'. However, successive studies for the European Commission claimed a permanent GDP boost of 1 per cent (in 1996) and 1.8 per cent (in 2002), while its 2007 analysis of the Single Market effect from 1992 to 2006 claimed a 2.15 per cent rise in GDP. Competition in government procurement had enabled savings of 10 to 30 per cent, it said. An internal paper for the Department for Business Innovation and Skills (BIS) from 2012 claimed that the European Commission's 2007 study, which gave no figures for individual countries, 'implies that the gain to UK GDP was in the region of £25 billion in 2006'.

In evidence to the House of Lords EU Select Committee in 2011, BIS said that

economic evidence shows that the single market has delivered substantial economic benefits. EU countries trade twice as much with each other as they would do in the absence of the single market programme. Given that, according to the OECD, a 10 percentage point increase in trade exposure is associated with a 4 per cent rise in income per capita, increased trade in Europe since the early 1980s may be responsible for around 6 per cent higher income per capita in the UK.

According to Vince Cable, the BIS Secretary, in a newspaper article in May 2012, this translated to a benefit of £3,500 for each household in the UK. A fellow Lib Dem minister in the same department was more circumspect in a parliamentary answer a few months earlier, however. Ed Davey wrote that

> available estimates show that the greater level of trade liberalisation achieved through the single market leads EU countries to trading currently twice as much with each other as they would do otherwise. As a result, the Single Market may be responsible for income gains in the UK between 2 per cent and 6 per cent, that is, between £1,100 and £3,300 a year per British household.

If ministers in the same pro-EU party and department of government cannot agree on the benefits of the Single Market, it would seem an impossible task to find any figure to command general respect.

At the other end of the spectrum, Patrick Minford, Professor of Applied Economics at Cardiff Business School, a supporter of the Better Off Out campaign to leave the EU, has estimated the cost of the EU to the British economy at between 11.2 per cent and 37.7 per cent of GDP, or £170 billion to £570 billion. Minford attributes the bulk of these costs to EU regulations, which he costs at between 6 and 25 per cent of GDP – a vast range and an upper figure far above other estimates. In 2013, the eurosceptic think tank Open Europe put the cost of the 100 most expensive EU regulations at

£27.4 billion a year, equivalent to just under 2 per cent of GDP, adding,

> it would be wrong to assume that these regulatory costs would magically disappear if the UK were to leave the EU. The UK government would probably want to keep a good number of these laws in part or in full – anti-discrimination laws, some health and safety rules, food safety standards, and so forth.

According to official government Impact Assessments, costs were exceeded by benefits. A closer look at these official assessments shows just how they are able to claim economic advantages, however. They strive to find benefits from effects such as a better work/life balance, reduction of accidents and higher productivity. Some of the assumptions made are wildly ambitious – for example the Impact Assessment on the EU's Climate and Energy Package. This stated that the cost would be £20.6 billion and the benefits between £9.2 billion and £242.1 billion. That's quite a margin of error and one that no private sector business would ever tolerate. The explanation for the unfeasible potential economic impact ranging from a £11.4 billion cost to a net benefit of £221.5 billion stated: 'Benefits will depend on other's actions and the emissions concentration trajectory the world is on. High end of range reflects world where EU action is pivotal in achieving a global deal.' This effectively meaningless cost-benefit analysis was signed off by the then responsible minister, former Secretary of State for Energy and Climate Change, Ed Miliband. No global deal is in sight.

Another attempt at placing a value on EU membership was made by the Confederation of British Industry in November 2013. It asserted that:

> It is not unreasonable to infer from a literature review that the net benefit arising from EU membership is somewhere in the region of 4–5 per cent of UK GDP or £62–£78 billion per year – roughly the economies of the North East and Northern Ireland taken together. This suggests that each UK citizen has benefited from EU membership to the tune of around £1,225 every year for the last forty years.

The CBI did not carry out any fresh research to arrive at this figure but analysed five earlier studies, including the CEPR paper from 2008 putting the benefit at 5 per cent of GDP along with others claiming benefits of 2.25 per cent, 2.1 per cent and 2 per cent of GDP, as well as one that claimed a net cost to consumers of 2.5 per cent. The pro-EU CBI's findings were clearly on the higher end of the consensus. Again, it showed the difficulty of reaching a single figure to sum up the EU's impact.

The exercise of attempting a crude cost-benefit analysis is frowned upon in Brussels for missing the point of the intangible benefits of nearly seventy years of peace and progress in Europe. The European Commission UK website argued:

It is far too simplistic and perverse to confine the European Union to a price tag. There are an array of benefits … that are difficult to quantify in cash: such as being part of a market of 500 million people, a cleaner and safer environment, and better security. It's like saying that it costs money to buy a house without saying that you need a house in the first place and that you would be in much worse situation without it!

Britain, of course, could move into a house that is either semi-detached from the EU by emulating Norway, or on its own plot by formally leaving the Single Market. The real question that will face voters in an in/out referendum is what would then be the impact on the national balance sheet. Several factors with important economic effects that contribute to a feeling of prosperity – notably jobs, immigration, investment and trade – are discussed in depth in other chapters of this book. But there are undoubtedly powerful arguments that the Single Market with its freedom of movement has positive economic benefits, leading to the position of UKIP's Nigel Farage quoted earlier that he would 'rather we were not slightly richer' in return for the ability to block migrants. The pro-EU *Financial Times* commentator Wolfgang Münchau has even argued that the entire economic argument is a red herring because Britain is bound to continue to benefit from free trade and free movement of capital even if it withdraws from the EU and its Single Market.

In macroeconomic terms, EU membership is virtually

irrelevant for a member state that is simultaneously large and not in the eurozone. The EU budget is tiny, and free trade and free capital movement would continue under any conceivable scenario. There may be reasons to stay in the EU, but whatever they are, they are not macroeconomic.

A feeling of prosperity is also about more than the ability of government and the economy to boost GDP. Work/life balance, social mobility, community cohesion, quality of the environment and personal health all contribute beyond the confines of an accountant's balance sheet. The independent think tank, the Legatum Institute, has been compiling an annual World Prosperity League table since 2007 based on eight main factors: economy, opportunity, governance, education, health, security, personal freedom and social capital. Britain was placed sixteenth in 2013, down three places on the previous year, slipping because of higher unemployment than more successful countries and falling investment, particularly in education – not a matter for the EU. Would the UK rise higher in the table outside the EU? The top three countries in the world according to the Legatum table on www.prosperity.com were Norway and Switzerland – two European nations outside the EU – followed by Canada. The top EU country, fourth-place Sweden, was one of those that, like the UK, kept out of the euro but proved that it was possible to be a member of the continental club and achieve that elusive feeling of prosperity regarded as the main aim of EU membership.

SOLIDARITY AND REGIONAL SUPPORT

IN Britain was instrumental in creating the EU's regional funding system to raise living standards, improve infrastructure and create jobs in poor European areas. The UK received €1.2 billion in 2013 from the €47 billion annual budget for regional spending in the twenty-eight EU countries.

OUT Britain would save its €5.8 billion annual payment towards EU regional funds and could choose how much to spend on UK projects. Non-EU member Norway pays a contribution towards poor eastern EU countries in a deal to smooth access to the Single Market, while Switzerland also makes a payment as part of its agreement with the EU.

KEY STATS Britain will receive €9.57 billion from 2014–20 in EU regional funds, made up of €457 million for Northern Ireland, €795 million for Scotland, €2,145 million for Wales and €6,174 million for England.[25] Britain received €10.6 billion in 2007–13 and paid in €36 billion.

Perched precariously on the top of Europe's tallest coastal cliff, the glass-bottomed viewing platform at Cabo Girão opened in 2012 and was the latest addition to the many EU-funded tourist attractions on the island of Madeira. The price tag for the platform, car park and café came to €2.5 million, made up of €2 million provided by so-called structural funds from Brussels and €500,000 of 'match-funding' from an island which had become addicted to EU cash. Madeira, a tiny outpost of Portugal in the Atlantic Ocean off the coast of Africa with a population of 267,000, has attracted €2 billion in EU regional funds in the past twenty-five years. In the rush to grab the cash, little thought was sometimes given to the practical implications of the building projects. The €38 million marina built for luxury ocean-going yachts lies empty with its entrance full of silt after waves cracked the sea wall; the accompanying €1.2 million restaurant complex was abandoned after rockfall from the cliffs above tore a hole in the roof; a €2.5 million business park on a remote hillside stands unused; the €670,000 oceanside helipad is rarely used.

Portugal has collected more than €60 billion in regional support funding from the EU since it joined in 1986 and went on a construction binge so notorious that it was given its own name, '*a política do betão*' (the politics of concrete), as politicians competed for vote-winning infrastructure projects. In 1989, Portugal had just 130 miles of motorways. Twenty years later, it had 1,777 miles – a lot of motorway in a country barely 300 miles long and 125 miles wide. It now has four times more miles of motorway per inhabitant than Britain and 60 per cent more than Germany. The irony is that, with the government forced to introduce road tolls as a condition of its €78 billion bailout deal following the collapse of the economy in the euro crisis, motorway use has plummeted. In 2013, the journey from Lisbon to Porto cost €22 in tolls, causing many drivers to take the smaller local roads and shun the EU-funded motorway system that was supposed to bring growth and jobs to the country.

The EU's seven-year budget for 2014–20 has earmarked a colossal €351 billion for regional projects, more than a third of all spending. As part of its agreement to join in 1973, Britain was instrumental in pushing for a system of funding to modernise Europe's poorest regions as a counterweight to the huge sums dished out under the Common Agricultural Policy that mainly supported traditional farming lifestyles. The aim was to make sure that no areas were left behind as cities grew more prosperous thanks to the increasing trade made possible by EU membership and consumed national infrastructure spending. Or, as the Treaty on European Union puts it, to 'work for the sustainable development of Europe based on balanced economic growth and ... promote economic, social and territorial cohesion, and solidarity among Member States'. The amounts of cash distributed by Brussels grew exponentially when the former Iron Curtain countries joined after 2004 but they have not been the biggest beneficiaries – from the beginning of their memberships until 2011, Spain, receiving the most so far, has secured €131.4 billion while Greece was handed €61.7 billion.

Britain's share of EU regional funding has dropped markedly as it became relatively more prosperous compared with the new member states but some regions have benefited significantly over the years. From the passenger terminal at John Lennon Airport to the 11,000-capacity Echo Arena and BT Convention

Centre in the former King's Dock, the revitalisa-
tion of Liverpool owes much to EU regional funding
for Merseyside worth £840 million in 2000–06 and
£268 million in the 2007–13 budget period. Under EU
rules for regenerating poorer areas in wealthier countries,
the money was given on condition that equal sums came
from the national authorities or private providers, meaning that the Liverpool Cruise Terminal – a huge floating
dock for ocean liners built in the Mersey in 2007 – was
paid for with £9 million from the UK government and
£8.6 million from the EU's European Regional
Development Fund. Liverpool's city centre and dock-
lands have been transformed from the desolation left by
the decline of the 1970s. The economic statistics show
an improvement, too – Merseyside's GDP in 2012 was
80.2 per cent of the European average, up from 70 per
cent in 1994, although the benchmark level dropped
when the former Communist countries joined in
2004. Liverpool is a tangible example of the impact of
European spending in the UK, even if some of the organisations that benefited were fined by Brussels in 2013 for
failing to display the EU logo on their projects. Yet the
British government has long argued for a fundamental
reform of regional spending, which would have meant
Merseyside never receiving a euro from Brussels.

As far back as 2003, Gordon Brown, then Chancellor
in the Labour government, argued that only the poorer
member countries – those with an economy worth
90 per cent or less of the EU average – should receive
regional funds. His logic for this was the philosophy of

subsidiarity, the EU term meaning that decisions should be taken at the most relevant level of government, either European, national or local. 'When the economic and social, as well as the democratic, arguments on structural funds now and for the future so clearly favour subsidiarity in action, there is no better place to start than by bringing regional policy back to Britain,' Brown wrote in *The Times*. The Open Europe eurosceptic think tank calculated that, with a threshold of 90 per cent of GDP for receiving cash from Brussels, Britain would have saved €4.6 billion from its gross contribution of €36 billion for regional funding in the 2007–13 budget period. In 2012, Mats Persson, director of Open Europe, said:

> In terms of an EU policy to target for reform, this is an open goal for Mr Cameron: it will save UK taxpayers billions, return powers from Brussels and allow the UK to run a far more effective domestic regeneration and regional policy, while still committing Britain to providing financial assistance to Europe's poorest regions.

In the face of overwhelming opposition from recipient countries, the Conservative and Liberal Democrat coalition gave up on this reform, however, to concentrate on cutting overall spending levels in the seven-year EU budget period from 2014 to 2020. A quick look at the potential impact from the cut in regional funding showed why reform stood no chance – the two main losers would have been Greece (a loss of €17 billion based on the 2007–13 figures) and Spain (a loss of €21.4 billion), at precisely the time when their own national economies were in dire straits because of the euro crisis and needed every cent of assistance to keep afloat.

David Cameron's decision to abandon any attempt to secure radical changes to regional funding during negotiations on the 2014–20 EU budget was reluctantly accepted by MPs on the Communities and Local Government Select Committee. But they urged the government not to give up on future reform of the main fund, called the European Regional Development Fund (ERDF). 'It is clear that withdrawing funding entirely from wealthier Member States is not supported for the 2014–20 ERDF round and we agree with the government's decision not to pursue it in negotiations,' the committee concluded in a report in July 2012. 'The government should, however, continue to put forward its arguments with the aim of securing enough support from other Member States for subsequent ERDF rounds.' Alarmingly the committee said that they could find no convincing evidence that the EU's enormous regional funding programmes had delivered demonstrable long-term benefits.

The EU's Structural and Cohesion Funds were set up to try and address some of the fundamental economic and social weaknesses of the least-developed regions of the EU. Although there have been some individual local successes it is difficult to prove that the funds have had a significant impact at a regional level. We looked at Cornwall and the Isles of Scilly, which ... has obtained the highest level of ERDF funding [in the UK] since 1994. This region faces particular problems which partly stem from its geographic position; EU funding will not resolve these issues. It can, however, still play a part in mitigating their effects – for instance through a Superfast Broadband project aimed at boosting productivity by connecting 10,000 businesses by 2014. However, as Professor Steve Fothergill [of the Centre for Regional Economic and Social Research at Sheffield Hallam University] told us, 'many of the problems we are dealing with in some of the less prosperous regions are deep-seated, and will take decades to turn round'. Although the majority of benefits are realised in later years, the evidence available to us suggests that ERDF 2007–13 has not yet made a significant impact. It is not even possible to conclude that the 2000–06 ERDF round has done so, because of the lack of robust evidence. The challenges facing regions such as Cornwall and the Isles of Scilly are profound, and ERDF can only provide part of any solution.

The cuts proposed by Gordon Brown and Open Europe, but resisted by almost every other EU nation, were taken up by campaigners from the Fresh Start group of Conservative MPs. In their manifesto for powers that David Cameron could try and take back from Brussels to national level as part of a renegotiation of Britain's relationship with the EU before holding a referendum, they wrote:

Regional Development Policy should be decentralised by limiting EU funds to those member states with GDP per head of less than 90 per cent of the EU average. This would provide more funds to those poorer member states, and end the needless recycling of funds among the wealthier member states. It could also result in a 15 per cent cut in the EU budget and enable wealthier member states to make their own decisions about how to support their own regions.

While this is the clear view of Conservative MPs, it is not shared by some of the UK regions themselves – and strongly opposed by the devolved Welsh government. The region of West Wales and the Valleys was the biggest recipient of regional funding in the 2007 to 2013 period with around €2 billion. Derek Vaughan, a Labour MEP, warned against regional funding for Wales becoming decided in Westminster and 'subjected to the whims of the Tory-Lib Dem government' instead of being allocated by the EU. In 2012, he wrote: 'It is a staggering leap of faith by Open Europe to believe that Wales would continue to receive fair and equal treatment under a coalition that has already shown its lack of commitment to Wales.'

A spokesman for the Welsh Government said:

Our position is clear – European regional policy should not be 'repatriated' to the UK. We are determined to ensure we secure the best possible deal for Wales. Structural funds have helped to mitigate the worst effects of the recession in Wales – helping nearly 41,000 people into work and helping to create 12,000 jobs and 2,450 enterprises – and the new programmes will allow us to build on the progress made to date in creating the environment for jobs and growth, helping to transform our communities and improving opportunities for people across Wales.

Not everyone believes that the EU funding for Wales has been worthwhile, however. Guto Bebb, the Welsh Conservative MP for Aberconwy, has compiled a list of 'white elephant' projects including Canolfan Cywain, a rural heritage centre in north Wales built with £900,000 of EU money plus match-funding. Opened in 2008 with an exhibition space, café and children's playground, it failed to pull in sufficient visitors and closed in 2012. 'The EU has created a series of white elephant projects,' Bebb told the *Sunday Telegraph*. 'These schemes, once built, have either closed or need large amounts of public funding to keep them open.' The EU's Court of Auditors has been very critical of the lack of rigorous controls on regional spending. Its report in July 2013 into the €65 billion spent on road projects in the EU since 2000 concluded that 'insufficient attention was paid to ensuring cost-effectiveness of the projects'. It found that motorways were often being built where regular express roads would have solved the traffic problems at just over half the price. Out of twenty-four road schemes audited, costs overran by 23 per cent on average and construction time overran by an average of nine months.

Calculated per 1,000 square metres of road, the lowest average costs were found in Germany of €287,043 while the highest were in Spain at €496,208. 'There is no evidence that this can be explained by labour costs,' the auditors remarked.

While the potential savings for the Treasury and taxpayer are massive from withdrawing from the EU and its regional funding programme, Britain would probably not entirely escape the obligation to fund Europe's poorer areas if it left the EU. If it emulated non-member Norway by joining the European Economic Area (EEA), giving it full access to the Single Market but no decisive say over the rules, Britain would be obliged to contribute to the EEA Grants. These are bilateral gifts from the EEA states (Norway, Iceland and Liechtenstein) to the newest countries of the EU. The amounts are negotiated every five years and are technically voluntary, although the EU expects payments in return for Single Market access. The amount Norway paid shot up tenfold when the first batch of former Communist countries joined the EU in 2004, and by another 25 per cent after Bulgaria and Romania joined in 2007. Norway paid €1.3 billion in 2004–08 and €1.8 billion in 2009–13, putting the non-EU member seventh among the net contributors to EU funding, although still paying much less than if it had actually been a full member.[26] Similarly Switzerland, from its position as a member of the European Free Trade Association (EFTA), agreed to pay 1 billion Swiss francs (around £654 million at 2012 prices) for projects in the ten countries which joined the EU in 2004, adding

181 million Swiss francs for Romania and 76 million Swiss francs for Bulgaria when they joined the EU in 2007.[27] When Croatia joined the EU in July 2013, Switzerland pledged 45 million Swiss francs for bilateral projects 'to strengthen economic and political relations' between the two countries. Various attempts have been made to estimate the amount that Britain would be obliged to pay towards projects in the EU's poorer states in return for continued access to the Single Market or Swiss-style bilateral trading conditions. In 2006, the Swiss government estimated that EEA membership would cost 32 per cent more, while full EU member-ship could cost six times as much, after receipts from Brussels, based on a gross contribution increase of 786 per cent. If it can be inferred from this that the UK would pay one-eighth of its overall fee to return to the EFTA relationship used by Switzerland, then the 2013 gross charge of £17.2 billion would be reduced to £2.15 billion, while the price of staying in the Single Market through the EEA would be around £2.8 billion a year.

SOVEREIGNTY

IN Britain shares sovereignty in a range of policy areas with the other twenty-seven EU nations to make decisions together on laws proposed by the European Commission, arguing its case in the European Parliament and Council of Ministers. It retains a veto over tax and defence matters and control over its currency. Parliament must implement EU law and obey rulings of the European Court of Justice.

OUT Parliament would have no obligation to follow EU law unless Britain joins the European Economic Area like Norway. Companies trading in Europe would still have to meet EU legal and technical rules, and comply with its competition policy, none of which the UK would have a say over. Britain would regain sovereignty over who crosses its borders, and other important areas including trade and agriculture policy and VAT.

KEY STATS 6.8 per cent of primary legislation (Statutes) and 14.1 per cent of secondary legislation (Statutory Instruments) implemented EU obligations between 1997 and 2009.[28] The government estimates that around 50 per cent of UK legislation with a significant economic impact originates from EU laws.[29]

For much of the last century, a British traveller's credentials to roam the world were contained in a distinctive hard-backed blue booklet bearing the title 'BRITISH PASSPORT' above the Royal crest on its cover. First introduced in 1920, the blue passport began to be phased out in 1988 and replaced with a smaller burgundy document standardised in size, colour and format with the other EU countries. It bears the title

'EUROPEAN UNION' above 'United Kingdom of Great Britain and Northern Ireland'. The idea of harmonising passports across Europe had been agreed as far back as December 1974 at a meeting of heads of government attended by Edward Heath. The details were finally signed off in June 1981 at a meeting of foreign ministers under another Conservative Prime Minister, Margaret Thatcher. The new European-style booklets removed the word 'British' from in front of the word 'Passport'. It was a tangible sign that British sovereignty was, literally, being erased. The new passports were gradually introduced over the next decade, coincidentally at the same time as the Maastricht Treaty created the notion of EU Citizenship – a status normally reserved for those living in a nation state. It seemed as if the deal Britain agreed in the 1970s to pool sovereignty to facilitate the Common Market was being extended to cover much wider areas of national life, touching on deep questions of identity and control over domestic affairs. This fuelled British fears about continental ambitions to create a United States of Europe, an ambition frequently mentioned at the time by Chancellor Helmut Kohl of Germany – and led to Thatcher's famous warning in her 1988 Bruges speech that 'we have not successfully rolled back the frontiers of the state in Britain only to see them reimposed at a European level, with a European superstate exercising a new dominance from Brussels'.

Clearly the actual British sovereign has not been replaced by the EU, although the institution of monarchy has benefited from various injections of European blood over the centuries from George of Hanover to Prince Albert of Saxe-Coburg and Gotha and Prince Philip of Greece and Denmark. Ultimate sovereignty in the UK, defined as independent legal authority over its territory, traditionally rests with Parliament. The EU changed this. Edward Heath explained that joining its forerunner, the European Economic Community, in 1973 would entail 'a sharing and an enlargement of individual national sovereignties in the general interest' and there was 'no question of any erosion of essential national sovereignty'. He was not so clear on what were to be regarded as 'essential' and non-essential areas. The European Court of Justice had already claimed ultimate jurisdiction over essential national sovereignty in areas of shared powers in a ruling in 1963. Another pro-European politician, the former deputy Labour Party leader Roy Hattersley, criticised Heath for refusing to acknowledge the sacrifices necessary to make Europe work: 'Nothing has more injured the idea of Britain in Europe than Edward Heath's foolish assurance (given at the time of our entry into the Common Market) that membership would involve no loss of sovereignty.' But speaking in 2000, Hattersley admitted that the pro-European case had been built on concealing the real fate of British national sovereignty:

What we did throughout all those years, all the Europeans, was say, let's not risk trying to make funda-mental changes by telling the whole truth, let's do it through public relations rather than real proselytising ...

spin the argument rather than expose the argument ...
Joining the European Community did involve significant
loss of sovereignty but by telling the British people that
was not involved, I think the rest of the argument was
prejudiced for the next twenty or thirty years.

Tony Blair shared Heath's view that sovereignty could
be shared and enlarged, and vowed to protect Britain's
interests by 'retaining the veto in areas where it is essential' while adding that 'sovereignty has to be deployed
for national advantage'. In the view of both Heath and
Blair, British sovereignty was not something that belonged
under lock and key in Whitehall or Westminster but could
be bartered and bargained in pursuit of national goals.
Although she did not spell it out at the time, this was
also what Thatcher practised when she agreed to sacrifice Britain's right of veto over dozens of policy areas by
allowing Qualified Majority Voting (QMV) to facilitate
decision-making among ministers from the member states
meeting in the European Council. 'We could never have
got the Single Market without an extension of majority
voting,' Thatcher commented in 1993. Every British Prime
Minister from Heath to Gordon Brown handed over more
national sovereignty to Brussels, until David Cameron's
government legislated in the EU Act of 2011 to hold a
referendum on the next substantial transfer of power.

There are several ways that national sovereignty has
been eroded by the EU. Ever more agreements are made
by QMV, meaning that in those policy areas Britain is no
longer able to stop EU laws by itself. A government minister

who opposes a new measure has to find enough ministers from other nations to form a blocking group, using
a formula based on national population levels. It was
not always like this. At the time that Britain joined,
when the European club was much smaller, there was
a gentleman's agreement that any one nation could call
time on any proposal that affected its 'very important
national interests'. But this agreement, known as the
Luxembourg Compromise, could not survive the expansion of the EU and died out in the 1980s. Few decisions
make it as far as a vote today because compromises are
usually agreed before that stage to avoid an acrimonious
showdown. Although renowned as being good at negotiations, Britain lost its record of never being outvoted on
a financial services policy in March 2013 when it failed
to prevent an EU cap on bankers' bonuses. In a sign of
Britain's waning influence and ability to form alliances
to safeguard an area of key national importance, not
one other member state sided with the UK. Qualified
Majority Voting has been steadily extended even to
matters of crucial national importance, such as the selec-
tion of the President of the European Commission and
the settlement of the EU's annual budget. In the past,
British Prime Ministers (John Major and Tony Blair)
used their power of veto to blackball ardent federal-
ists (both from Belgium) for the top job in the EU
bureaucracy. Such a veto is no longer possible because
the appointment was made subject to QMV by the
Lisbon Treaty, along with the final decision on the EU's
annual budget.

The idea of the Luxembourg Compromise has been suggested by the Fresh Start group of Conservative MPs in the form of an 'emergency brake' in their Mandate for Reform to guide David Cameron on the powers he should try and win back from the EU ahead of a referendum. In November 2013, they wrote:

> There is a very real issue of a sovereign government being outvoted in Brussels under Qualified Majority Voting, and a law being foisted upon a nation against the will of its government and people, and it must be addressed. An emergency brake procedure should be introduced, modelled on the so-called Luxembourg Compromise. Under this provision, a member state that considers an EU proposal to be a threat to a fundamental national interest could refer that proposal to the European Council where unanimity, and hence a national veto, would apply.

Such a move is regarded as a backwards step in Brussels that would bring decision-making to a halt by effectively making every single measure again subject to unanimity and endless negotiation.

British sovereignty over making and enforcing its own laws has also been chipped away by the European Court of Justice. This body, based in Luxembourg and consisting of twenty-eight judges – one from each EU member state – is the supreme arbiter of European law, giving it a decisive say over increasing aspects of British life, such as justice and home affairs policies under the Lisbon

Treaty of 2009. Sometimes areas of national life which are not supposed to be controlled by the EU have been ordered to change by the judges in Luxembourg. One of these was car insurance. In a ruling on gender equality in 2011 based on a test case brought by a Belgian consumer group, the ECJ judged that it was illegal to exempt car insurers from discrimination on the basis of sex. This meant that the government had to change British law by issuing a Statutory Instrument (SI 2012/2992 amending the Equality Act) to stop insurers offering lower premiums to women drivers from December 2012. Calling the ruling 'utter madness', Sajjad Karim, a Conservative MEP, said:

> It is a statistical reality that young men have more car accidents than women so it should be reflected in their premiums. Once again we have seen how an activist European Court can over-interpret the treaty. Unelected judges have overruled the will of democratically elected MEPs and governments; is it any wonder people are so disenchanted with the EU?

Another knock-on effect was on the pensions industry, where it became illegal for providers to continue their usual practice of offering higher annuity rates to men because they lived fewer years in retirement than women. The ruling was welcomed as 'an important step towards putting the fundamental right of gender equality into practice' by Viviane Reding, the EU's Justice Commissioner. 'A modern insurance company should not distinguish between women and men,' she added. Whatever one thought about the change, it was a clear example of British law being directed by the judges in Luxembourg – as a result of a court case brought by Belgium.

Concerns over the circumvention of national sovereignty were epitomised by the introduction of the Working Time Directive in 1993. Britain had opted out of the Social Chapter of the Maastricht Treaty to avoid the EU setting rules on domestic working conditions. Jacques Delors, then European Commission President, simply bypassed the Social Chapter by proposing the Working Time Directive under a different legal route, health and safety law, which was agreed by Qualified Majority Voting by eleven votes to one, with only Britain against. This legislation stipulated maximum weekly working hours as well as daily and weekly rest periods and minimum holidays. There was already an understandable sense of Britain being bumped into accepting the directive before a series of rulings by the ECJ then dramatically expanded the application of the EU law with massive extra costs to employers. The Simap judgment in 2000 added on-call time to working hours calculations; the Jaeger judgment of 2003 ruled that time spent asleep at the workplace (such as junior doctors at hospital) counted as working time; the Stringer judgment of 2009 meant that paid annual leave continued to accrue when workers were off sick, even if they were off sick all year; and the Pereda judgment of 2009 ruled that if an employee fell sick just before taking annual leave, he could take the holiday that overlapped with his sickness at a later date. The EU does not have formal powers over national healthcare systems and yet the NHS alone faced huge extra costs, with the directive blamed for much of its £1 billion annual bill for agency workers to cover gaps in rotas.

The ECJ has long been viewed by eurosceptics as having the overtly political objective of forging greater EU integration due to its mandate not only to clarify the law but also to uphold the European treaties and their founding principle to create 'ever closer union' contained in the first line of the original Treaty of Rome of 1957. This prompted David Cameron to take up a call from his backbenchers for the commitment to be dropped. 'The European treaty commits the member states to "lay the foundations of an ever closer union among the peoples of Europe",' Cameron said in his Bloomberg speech.

This has been consistently interpreted as applying not to the peoples but rather to the states and institutions compounded by a European Court of Justice that has consistently supported greater centralisation. We understand and respect the right of others to maintain their commitment to this goal. But for Britain – and perhaps for others – it is not the objective. And we would be much more comfortable if the treaty specifically said so, freeing those who want to go further, faster, to do so, without being held back by the others.

This attempt to draw a line in the sand to protect national sovereignty found support from a founding member state, the Netherlands, which declared after its own review of EU policy that 'the time of an "ever closer union" in every possible policy area is behind us'. Unanimity of all twenty-eight member states would be necessary to change that fundamental part of the EU treaties, however.

If Britain cannot renegotiate a less intrusive relationship with the EU, leaving would not necessarily see sovereignty fully restored to Parliament. Partly that is because, as explored in later chapters, no country can exist in isolation from the international rules that govern cross-border activities like finance, trade, travel and transportation. Partly it is also because the UK will not become completely detached from Europe in the event of Brexit. As discussed in the Democracy chapter, if the UK wants to stay fully inside the Single Market after leaving the EU it will have to be in the European Economic Area like Norway. While this will restore national sovereignty over agriculture, fisheries, justice and home affairs, regional funding and trade, Parliament would have to agree to accept all EU laws related to the Single Market without having a decisive say over them. Outside the EEA, if Britain tried something like the Swiss system of bilateral deals with Brussels on different areas of interest like trade and air travel, this would offer a greater return to national sovereignty, although in practice many international standards for activities like farming, consumer protection and the environment would still be set in Brussels without British input.

You have to go all the way back to Harold Macmillan

to find a Prime Minister prepared to explain candidly what joining the European club would really mean for British sovereignty. 'It is true of course that political unity is the central aim of those European countries and we would naturally accept that ultimate goal,' he wrote in a pamphlet in 1962, setting out his reasons for making Britain's first, unsuccessful, application for membership. 'In renouncing some of our own sovereignty we would receive in return a share of the sovereignty renounced by other members.' The most eloquent modern explanation of why it makes sense to share sovereignty to achieve national goals in today's more complicated world and much larger European Union came from a judicial source. The life story of Sir Konrad Schiemann, Britain's former judge at the European Court of Justice, owes much to the peaceful system of European cooperation created after the Second World War, a conflict which left him an orphan in his native Berlin. Brought by an uncle to grow up in England, he studied at Cambridge, became a High Court judge and rose to the pinnacle of British society as a member of the Privy Council. 'We no longer live in a time when the military and economic might of the UK was such that the government could hope to achieve whatever it desired by threats. Gunboat diplomacy has gone,' Schiemann wrote in an essay for Regent's University in 2013.

The achievement of our national aims requires the cooperation of other governments, just as the achievement of their national aims requires our cooperation. We cannot all do exactly what we want, because we do not all want the same things. Progress is made by giving up one desideratum in order to achieve another. This involves making choices difficult for all parties – a task which is made impossible if each party relies on a concept of sovereignty which implies that it must be free of all constraints and allowed to do whatever it wants.

Schiemann argued that it would be inefficient and ineffective to withdraw from multilateral bodies like the EU and try to achieve national aims by negotiating bilaterally with every country on every issue. 'The structure of the EU is designed to facilitate the inevitable compromises,' he wrote, dismissing the idea of an 'emergency brake' to pull out of unwanted policies.

For shared sovereignty to be effectively exercised requires mutual trust and mutual commitment. If you wish to obtain the certainty that your partner will be bound by the agreement even when he or she finds it inconvenient, then you have to live with the fact that you must agree to be bound by it even when you find it inconvenient.

Schiemann appealed for debate about sovereignty to be rooted in the real world where some countries are more powerful than others and all have their own national interests. Even the most powerful cannot achieve everything they want without cooperating with others.

A state's domestic law may permit it to export sausages with a large bread content, or beer with a small hop content, or indeed nuclear detritus or other refuse. But this is of no practical value unless other states permit the import of those goods. So mutual agreement has to be reached ... A state's domestic laws may limit radiation emissions or prescribe air quality of a particular purity, but this is of limited practical value if emissions or air of inferior quality comes in from the state next door. So equivalent standards are desirable. A state may wish to encourage its companies to establish subsidiaries in other states, but this is of little practical value unless the other states in question allow the establishment of such subsidiaries. So mutual recognition is required.

The major achievement of the EU has been setting up a mechanism for arriving at policy decisions which bind everyone, he concluded.

You have to take the rough with the smooth, and you have to accept compromise ... The most effective way for the UK to achieve what it wishes to achieve is by seeking to persuade others that they are likely to achieve more of what they want if they do not stand in the way of the UK achieving what it wants. This is more easily done within the EU than outside it. If we are outside, those countries inside will devote their energies to doing deals with their partners inside the Union and are likely – politely or less politely – to ignore us.

Schiemann is persuasive – that's his job as an advocate. But the key issue for many British voters is that the EU has gone too far and claimed too much jurisdiction over national life. Subsidiarity – the EU's technical term for power being exercised at the appropriate local, national or European level – has never been rigorously applied to devolve decision-making. Instead, Brussels empire builders have grabbed national sovereignty in a game of thrones that many Europeans, not just the British, feel they did not sign up for. Schiemann's eloquent argument for pooling sovereignty cannot be faulted for its logic, only for its application. The impact of the European Union's ever-widening range of powers over national life causes legitimate concerns about the sacrifice of sovereignty that is demanded and touches on deep feelings of national identity. Brussels also wields power in sectors where it formally has little, for example in healthcare with the huge costs to the NHS of the Working Time Directive. The one-way transfer of sovereignty also causes alarm that a power-hungry central authority is competing with national parliaments in a zero sum game rather than cooperating with them. This all helps to explain why there are so many 'swing voters' in Britain, who polls suggest would support continued membership if the scope of EU power was scaled back and British sovereignty re-enhanced in a renegotiation. Nobody can argue for complete sovereignty in today's inter-connected world, where compromises have to be struck internationally to enable global systems of finance, travel and trade to function. The question is the degree to which Britain needs to be committed to integration in a political organisation that demands 'ever closer union' to achieve national goals. Opinion polls suggest that if the government can get the balance of sovereignty right with the EU, the British will vote to stay in, whereas too much accumulation of power in Brussels – and Luxembourg – will push the UK away.[30]

TRADE

IN The EU has sole responsibility for negotiating international trade agreements on behalf of its twenty-eight members and has concluded recent deals with Canada, Singapore and South Korea, with the big prizes of the US, Japan and India in the pipeline. No tariffs or quotas apply to goods moving between EU states and a common tariff is applied to goods entering from outside.

OUT Britain can negotiate its own preferential trade agreements, take up its own seat at the World Trade Organization, regain the power to decide its own import duties and explore a wider Commonwealth trading deal. It could continue to deal on preferential terms with the EU through a Free Trade Agreement, or on the same terms as a full member if it is in the European Economic Area.

KEY STATS The EU is by far Britain's biggest trading partner, accounting for 45.8 per cent of UK goods and services exports (£224 billion) in 2012 and 50.5 per cent of imports (£265 billion).[31] Britain's next biggest trading partner is the US with £81.6 billion of exports and £49.7 billion of imports in 2012.[32] Britain recorded its highest monthly trade gap in goods with the EU in November 2013 with imports (£18.8 billion) exceeding exports (£12.1 billion) by £6.7 billion in that month.[33] For UK exporters and importers, Germany is the main EU partner followed by Netherlands and France.

Lye Cross Farm's premium cheese made by Alvis Brothers of north Somerset sits at a constant temperature of 8–12°C in their warehouse for a year to replicate the same gentle ageing conditions of the famous local caves originally used to store and mature cheddar. The company combines traditional methods with a very modern approach to sales which has seen exports grow from 4 to 25 per cent of their output in just a few years. Not only do they sell cheese to the French but Lye Cross Farm is also a big hit in South Korea, where sales were up 50 per cent in 2012. Tim Harrap, the company's head of collaboration, puts the export success down to a combination of factors, including the appeal of the Union Jack on the wrapper and trade fairs run by UK Trade & Industry (UKTI), the government's trade promotion body, as well as personal contacts. But he gives the main credit for being able to break into international markets to the European Union, not just to the Single Market but to its food quality schemes, particularly the Protected Designation of Origin (PDO) label, awarded to Lye Cross Farm for their West Country Farmhouse Cheddar, verifying its authenticity and provenance. This gave it extra kudos in the status-obsessed Far East market. 'Korea is a great place as there is a strong interest in Britain and its culture, so the UK's imported products are much sought after by consumers,' said Harrap. 'The biggest driver of this was the European Union–South Korea Free Trade Agreement. Although the tariffs on cheese were not cut straight away they are reducing over the years. We are up against the New Zealand product but there is no free trade agreement between New Zealand and South Korea.' Harrap has travelled extensively promoting British cheese as part of UK and EU trade missions around the globe, having watched other local cheddar producers that did not diversify into foreign sales go out of business. Export success for him depends on a combination of British pluck and EU muscle. 'It seems to me that whilst the British are navel gazing the world is moving on apace – we cannot afford to pull up the drawbridge.'

In the twenty years before Britain joined the EEC in 1973, the proportion of UK trade (total of imports and exports) with the original six member nations rose from 13 to 21 per cent. In the twenty years following accession, British trade with these six countries more than doubled to 44 per cent.[34] This was hardly surprising given the thousands of common standards and rules adopted by the member states to smooth trade between them, as well as the common external tariff to deter competition from outside their Customs Union. An internal UK government paper released under Freedom of Information rules from 2005 put the boost of EU membership for trade between member states at 40 per cent while the loss of trade with countries outside the EU due to its Customs Union was said to be 5 per cent.[35] The question now, however, is whether it is time to refocus elsewhere given Europe's relatively low growth prospects compared to other parts of the world. In an article in *The Times* in May 2013 explaining why he would vote to leave the EU, the former Chancellor of the Exchequer Lord Lawson argued that the general lowering of global tariffs and other barriers through successive rounds of World Trade Organization liberalisation now made EU membership unnecessary from a trade perspective. To make his point, he said that UK exports to the EU had risen in cash terms by 40 per cent over the decade but that exports to the EU from countries outside it had gone up by 75 per cent. 'The heart of the matter is that the relevant economic context nowadays is not Europe but globalisation, including global free trade, with the World Trade Organization as its monitor,' he concluded. He also warned that British businesses were too focused on Europe, a continent in slow decline, and were therefore missing great export opportunities in the developing world, especially Asia. The EU had served its 'historic purpose' and was now 'past its sell-by date', he argued. The facts bear out Lawson's case on the EU's inward-looking approach to trade. In the Mercosur group of nations in South America, 16 per cent of exports are to each other and 84 per cent further afield; in the Asean group of countries in South East Asia, 25 per cent of exports are within the region; and in Nafta in North America (US, Canada and Mexico) 51 per cent are inter-regional.[36] In the EU, meanwhile, 65 per cent of exporting is between member nations. This over-reliance on intra-EU trade comes at a time of general economic decline both in absolute terms and relative to the rest of the world. Europe's share of world merchandise trade has fallen from its peak of 50.9 per cent in 1973 to 45.4 per cent in 1993 and 37.9 per cent in 2010.[37]

Lye Cross Farm, however, is one British business that owes much not just to the EU's Single Market but also to its sole responsibility for negotiating preferential Free Trade Agreements (FTAs) with countries and regions further afield. The FTA with South Korea, which came into force in July 2011, had an immediate impact on British trade. UK goods exports to the world's fifteenth-largest economy grew by 82 per cent in 2012 to £4.9 billion and services grew by 5 per cent to £1.5 billion.[38] The South Korea FTA was the most extensive trade deal ever struck by the EU at the time and came after a 'lost decade' when Brussels was more focused on trying to secure a global trade liberalisation agreement under the WTO's Doha Round of talks that began in 2001. While these negotiations were stalled for years, other developed trading nations like the United States and Australia pushed on with making FTAs that fuelled frustration among eurosceptics at the apparent inaction of the European Commission and led to trade becoming a key argument in favour of leaving the EU. In the same time that the EU managed only one modern FTA with South Korea, New Zealand concluded eight trade deals including with China, Malaysia and Thailand. 'We don't want to be stuck inside a Customs Union that prohibits us from making our own trade deals with the rest of the world – the growing parts of the world,' Nigel Farage told UKIP's annual conference in 2012.

After the renegotiation of a simple free trade deal with the European Union, we would like to see Britain thinking bigger. There is a group of countries out there that represent nearly a third of the population of the globe, where they speak English, have common law, are our real friends in the world. We would like to extend free trade to include the Commonwealth. That is the way forward.

If Britain were to leave the EU, its first port of call for new trading relationships would be the so-called Anglosphere (basically, the Commonwealth plus the US). As UKIP policy stated:

UKIP will seek to establish a Commonwealth Free Trade Area (CFTA) with the fifty-three other Commonwealth countries. The Commonwealth Business Council estimates that a CFTA would account for more than 20 per cent of all international trade and investment, facilitating annual trade exchanges worth more than $1.8 trillion and direct foreign investment worth about $100 billion. Yet the Commonwealth has been shamefully betrayed and neglected by previous governments. Commonwealth nations share a common language, legal and democratic systems, account for a third of the world's population and a quarter of its trade, with the average age of a citizen just twenty-five years. India, for example, will soon become the second largest world economy and Britain should not be tied to the dead political weight of the European Union, but retain its own friendly trading and cultural links.

Europe is getting older and growing less, both economically and demographically, than the rest of the world. The EU had two countries among the world's most populous twenty nations in 2000: Germany in twelfth place with 82.3 million and France in twentieth place with 59.3 million. The Commonwealth had four in the top ten: India in second place with 1.02 billion people;

Pakistan seventh with 142.7 million; Bangladesh eighth with 138 million; and Nigeria tenth with 114.7 million. By 2050 there are forecast to be no current EU countries among the world's biggest twenty, although Turkey makes nineteenth place with 97.8 million people. India will become the world's most populous country with 1.53 billion inhabitants and the Commonwealth will have five in the top twenty: Pakistan fourth; Nigeria sixth; Bangladesh seventh; and Uganda seventeenth.[39]

The World Economics organisation found in 2012 that the Commonwealth's share of global GDP had already overtaken that of Britain's major partners in Europe. Their researchers plotted real terms GDP and growth for the eight nations (excluding the UK) which have been members of the EU since 1973, and compared it to the growth rate for Commonwealth countries and also with the eurozone. They found that the Commonwealth had come from a long way behind to outperform the EU8 in terms of share of world GDP and was poised to do the same with the eurozone. Real terms average annual growth for the eurozone was forecast to rise by 2.7 per cent from 2012 until 2017 and for the Commonwealth by 7.3 per cent, using International Monetary Fund figures. 'Whilst joining the EU may have been a good thing for the UK for a number of reasons, it is clear that in sheer market growth terms, the Commonwealth is proving the more dynamic economic grouping,' said World Economics. 'The potential for future market growth appears very limited in the EU, whereas the potential is still vast in the Commonwealth.'

Population growth in the Commonwealth is set to be twice as rapid as in the eurozone up until 2050.

The Commonwealth would not be the only option available to Britain if it left the EU and was free to make its own global trade deals again. The other obvious place to look would be across the Atlantic to North America, where Canada, Mexico and the US concluded the North American Free Trade Agreement (Nafta) in 1994. The benefits in terms of increased trade were huge in the following decade, leading some Republican politicians to suggest that the UK could also benefit by joining. *The Economist* noted that Nafta looked just like the sort of arrangement that Britain always wanted the EU to be, i.e. 'a giant free-trade area linking sovereign countries, without any common body of law, or any notion of developing a common foreign policy'. The only snag, the magazine added, was that the UK signed over its ability to negotiate entry into Nafta when it joined the EU.

While an independent UK would be much smaller than the EU and have less clout in international trade negotiations on its own, it would not be a minnow. It is the world's tenth largest merchandise exporter, with $406 billion worth in 2010, a quarter the value of China's and a third the value of the US's. Britain is the sixth biggest importer of goods, with $560 billion, behind the US, China, Germany, Japan and France. But when it comes to the trade in commercial services, the UK actually exports more in dollar value than China, $227 billion compared to $170 billion, putting it in third place behind the US and Germany.[40] In recent years, however, the case for Britain leaving the EU to make Free Trade Agreements of its own has weakened. That is because the European Commission finally accepted the futility of chasing the Doha world deal and set out an ambitious programme of its own, following the South Korea FTA with Colombia and Peru, and reaching agreement in 2013 with Singapore and Canada, the latter forecast to increase bilateral trade in goods and services by a fifth to €25.7 billion a year. The British economy is estimated to benefit from the Canada deal by £1.3 billion a year. 'Over the next two years, 90 per cent of world demand will be generated outside the EU,' the commission's trade directorate said in June 2013.

> That is why it is a key priority for the EU to open up more market opportunities for European business by negotiating new Free Trade Agreements with key countries. If we were to complete all our current free trade talks tomorrow, we would add 2.2 per cent to the EU's GDP or €275 billion. In terms of employment, these agreements could generate 2.2 million new jobs or [an] additional 1 per cent of the EU total workforce.

A trade agreement with the US would stimulate European GDP by €65 billion, with Japan by €43 billion and with India by €3.8 billion, the Commission forecast, with further significant productivity gains to follow. As a trading nation, Britain, with 11.5 per cent of all EU exports and 14.5 per cent of EU imports, could expect to benefit disproportionately from this potential windfall. Success in these ambitions would negate a big part of the argument for British withdrawal, namely that the EU is too sclerotic and inward-looking to conclude better deals than Britain could achieve on its own. The real potential game-changer in the trade argument is the proposed deal with the US, known as the Transatlantic Trade and Investment Partnership (TTIP), which is why David Cameron was so keen to stand alongside President Obama to announce the start of the talks in July 2013. TTIP is forecast to boost UK exports to the US by between 1.2 and 2.9 per cent, benefit the British economy by between £4 billion and £10 billion a year, and set down regulatory benchmarks for the rest of the world.[41] A comprehensive EU–US deal, in parallel with a Japan agreement, following Canada, Singapore and South Korea, would effectively kill the argument that Britain has to leave the EU to secure its international trade future. A further argument in favour of sticking with the EU is the view both within the European Commission and the UK government's Department for Business, Innovation and Skills that Britain would not automatically be able to continue with the Free Trade Deals negotiated by the EU if it were to end its membership. John Clancy, EU Trade spokesman, said:

If a country leaves the EU, European law becomes inapplicable. This includes trade agreements between the EU and third countries. The UK would therefore not benefit from any preference granted by a third state to the EU. Reversely the UK would be free to define its own external customs tariff with all third countries.

David Cameron must be hoping that the French do not wreck the TTIP as they did the last attempt at an EU–US trade deal in 1998. Keen as always to protect its farmers from competition, France feared that agricultural goods would get dragged into the negotiations, despite repeated promises that they were not on the table. 'We do not want our American friends to come and stick their noses into the way we organise Europe,' said the then French finance minister, Dominique Strauss-Kahn, later managing director of the International Monetary Fund. French President Jacques Chirac accused Leon Brittan, the British commissioner in charge of EU trade, of

> going off on his own, like a big man, to negotiate a free trade zone between the United States and Europe without a mandate ... It is absurd, and, I have to say, it is indecent. We have the World Trade Organization, we all wanted it and we all signed it. And this is where commercial agreements should be negotiated.

French farmers are unhappy about any prospect of agriculture being included in the TTIP after Canada won the right to export 80,000 metric tons of pork and 50,000 metric tons of beef free of duties to the EU under its agreement. 'The European Commission is blindly preparing for a deal with the United States that will hasten the bankruptcy of farms and jobs in the sector,' said FNB, the French beef farm federation, in 2013. The TTIP talks continue.

If Britain were to leave the EU, it could regain its international trade mandate and stay inside the Single Market by following Norway into the European Economic Area (EEA). If the EEA was rejected, then Britain would try for a Free Trade Agreement with the EU like Switzerland, preferably with access for both goods and services. This could be overseen by something similar to the Trade Committee for the EU–South Korea FTA which has fifteen members, five from each side and five neutrals, as well as six specialised committees of experts in particular fields: trade in goods, sanitary and phytosanitary, customs, trade in services, sustainable development, and outward processing zones. There are also seven sectoral working groups. Instead of the European Court of Justice (ECJ), there is a system of consultations to resolve disputes and failing that, matters go before a three-person arbitration panel, made up of members of the Trade Committee chaired by one of the independents. That is quite a reduction from the ECJ with its 1,991 staff and its 2014 annual budget of €355 million.[42]

If no FTA was agreed, however, Britain's trading relationship with the EU would then be based on the general rules of the World Trade Organization. It would not mean exorbitant new tariffs for all British exporters although some sectors would suffer badly. Cars would face a 10 per cent import duty, for example, as discussed in the Investment chapter, in the unlikely event that pressure from the German government in support of its exporters did not prevail. The arguments for keeping close trading links with the EU are many and varied, and generally accepted by eurosceptics. Campaigners for Brexit argue that there is little prospect of a complete breakdown in relations and so a preferential UK-EU FTA is a strong likelihood, given the present close and mutually advantageous trading relationship. Daniel Hannan, a Conservative MEP and one of the most persuasive campaigners for Britain to pull out of the EU, wrote:

I have yet to meet a British eurosceptic who wants to withdraw from the European market. Such people may exist but, in all the years that I've campaigned against the current system, I've never come across them. What eurosceptics want, rather, is to withdraw from the EU's political structures while retaining trade links – along the lines of what Switzerland does, though with some modifications. This point is worth stressing, because supporters of EU membership have taken to arguing against a proposition that no one is seriously suggesting, namely the idea that Britain, a maritime and mercantile nation, should cut all ties to her European allies ... It is sometimes suggested that, if Britain withdrew from the EU's political structures, it would face economic sanctions from the other members. I don't believe it: trade barriers would be self-defeating. In 2013, the UK overtook France to become Germany's single biggest export destination. We run a structural trade deficit with the EU (though not with the rest of the world), buying more than we sell. On the day we left the customs union, we would become easily its largest market, larger than the second and third largest (the US and Japan) combined. Why would anyone want to restrict cross-channel trade?

The UK's large trade deficit with the EU (UK imports exceeded exports by £41 billion in 2012) means that the continent would have more to lose in a trade war than Britain. But if Britain was outside the EU and EEA, agreement on free trade with the member states on services would be less certain than for goods. Within the overall trade deficit in 2012, the UK ran a surplus in services meaning that exports were £13.6 billion more than imports, giving the EU less of an incentive to agree a free trade deal on services – as discussed further in the chapter on the City – which in turn could harm the British economy given the size of its service sector. The government has said that British GDP could be boosted by up to 7 per cent by 'completing the Single Market' in services by breaking down the EU's remaining internal trade barriers. On the one hand, it is an indictment of the resistance to market opening in EU countries that much still remains to be done on things like the recognition of professional qualifications to open up competition on services. On the other hand, it is another argument in favour of Britain staying inside the EU to push for reform rather than leaving and removing pressure on recalcitrant governments across the Channel to give UK services a better chance to compete for business there.

SECTORS

THE CITY AND FINANCE

IN London is the undisputed financial centre of the EU despite the UK staying out of the euro. A strong British voice at the table during decisions on laws proposed by the European Commission and amended by MEPs helps to protect the City's competitiveness.

OUT Free of EU controls, the City could become an offshore financial centre to Europe like Singapore or Hong Kong to Asia. But if the UK fails to retain complete access to the Single Market for financial services, there could be an exodus of international players from London.

KEY STATS Britain has a 70 per cent market share of financial services in Europe. 78 per cent of all foreign exchange trades in the EU and 85 per cent of hedge fund management takes place in the City. Financial services accounted for 7.9 per cent of UK GDP and 12 per cent of tax receipts in 2012.[43]

When a Frenchman was appointed as European Commissioner for the Single Market and Financial Services for the first time in fifty years, Nicolas Sarkozy, the French President, declared that the British were 'the big losers' in the five-yearly carve-up of top EU jobs in 2009. 'I want the world to see the victory of the European model, which has nothing to do with the excesses of financial capitalism,' said Sarkozy, who blamed the global economic crisis on the 'free-wheeling Anglo-Saxon' model of financial market practices. Michel Barnier, the former French Foreign Minister chosen for the commissioner role, was quick to try and reassure a nervous City of London over fears that he would unleash a barrage of EU legislation not merely to clip its wings but to bring it down. 'I plan to work with everybody. I'm not an ideologist. I'm very practical. Everybody needs to calm down,' he said. A British eurocrat was installed as director-general of Barnier's department to ease government concerns. Five years on, Barnier's directorate had produced one of the most extensive legislative programmes ever seen in one term of a European Commissioner but many of the new laws were limited to the eighteen nations in the eurozone. Much of the legislation and policy was aimed at preventing a repeat of the near break-up of the euro in 2010–12 and Britain ensured that it opted out of the most demanding calls on national sovereignty made in the proposed EU Banking Union. These included the Single Supervisory Mechanism under the European Central Bank to keep an eye on the biggest banks in the eurozone and the proposed Single Resolution Mechanism for winding up a failing eurozone bank. A host of other measures were also brought in for all twenty-eight EU nations, however. Measures for closer supervision and annual recommendations by the European Commission about national budgets in the European Semester programme, led to the extraordinary spectacle of the Irish Budget being sent to Brussels and discussed in the finance committee of the German Bundestag before it reached the floor of the Dáil. Again, Britain kept some distance from this policy by refusing to hand over details of its Budget until Parliament heard them first.

Although many in the City grumbled about extra controls and safeguards, Barnier was not the monster some had feared. The real problem that emerged during his tenure for the UK was the growing realisation that the euro club was growing in regulatory strength. Far from losing members as seemed possible during the height of the euro crisis – with huge bailout loans provided to Greece, Portugal, Ireland and Cyprus in return for drastic economic reforms – Latvia joined the Single Currency in 2014 and others including Poland are queuing up to follow it. This will only increase their tendency to club together to back EU legislation and policy primarily to benefit their own interests. Of the twenty-eight EU members, only the UK and Denmark have treaty-based opt-outs from the euro, although Sweden is likely to avoid joining for the foreseeable future. Even without any new members, the eighteen eurozone countries have an unbeatable qualified majority to win votes in the European Council from November 2014 when new rules from the Lisbon Treaty come into force stipulating that a decision can only pass with 55 per cent of the members and 65 per cent of the EU population (the eurozone had 65.9 per cent in 2014).

David Cameron's first stab at protecting the UK's financial services industry from a eurozone caucus was a spectacular flop. The Prime Minister told an EU summit in December 2011 that he wanted several safeguards in exchange for agreeing to the Fiscal Compact, a new set of German-inspired economic rules to limit national debts and deficits aimed mainly at eurozone countries. He wanted a guarantee that greater fiscal coordination in the eurozone would not distort the Single Market; a legal protocol to protect the City of London from excessive regulation including the ability to enforce higher bank capital requirements than the suggested EU maximum; agreement that the European Banking Authority would stay in London; and protection from EU regulation for US financial institutions based in London that do not trade with Europe. The other EU leaders refused, partly because not enough time was spent building up allies around the table before the meeting, and partly because the details were not seen as directly relevant to the subject in hand, namely the coordination of national budgets. The rest of the EU, with the exception of the Czech Republic, simply ignored Cameron and went ahead with a treaty between themselves to implement the Fiscal Compact, vowing to make it full EU law by 2018. Cameron's failed repatriation of powers was essentially about restoring a veto to financial services regulation. In common with many aspects of the Single Market, the veto was replaced with Qualified Majority Voting to speed up decision-making and overcome vested national interests under rule changes agreed to by Margaret Thatcher. But Cameron had support from the industry for his tough stance – 70 per cent of managers at UK finance firms told a poll in December 2011 that they agreed with the statement: 'The UK government needs to renegotiate existing EU treaties to safeguard the City of London, limiting agreements to trade and association only.' And 68 per cent agreed that: 'The UK government should take back more control from the EU over financial regulation and governance even if it risks compromising the possibility of easier access to other European countries.'[44]

Britain's next attempt at protecting the City from hostile eurozone-inspired laws was much more successful. During negotiations for the first stage of a Banking Union for the eurozone in December 2012, giving the European Central Bank responsibility for supervising the biggest banks in the Single Currency area, George Osborne secured a new 'double-majority' system for decisions by the European Banking Authority, the organisation that regulates most, smaller, EU banks. When a new rule is agreed, there will have to be a majority by voting weight of all EU members, plus a simple unweighted majority of the eurozone 'outs' and 'ins'. If a majority of the eurozone 'outs' do not like a new banking rule, they can block it. As Robert Peston of the BBC said on his blog:

Although this double-majority voting system for the EBA sounds boringly procedural, it could prove to be very significant. It could provide an important blueprint to preserve the UK's voting voice and weight on the future of the Single Market, as and when the eurozone evolves into an even more unified political bloc. It implies that the UK might be able to co-exist in the European Union with a currency union that becomes a political union.

The Fresh Start group of Conservative MPs are urging Cameron to negotiate an extension of the 'double-majority lock' to avoid the eighteen eurozone countries writing the rules for all twenty-eight EU members.

There are two schools of thought for what happens to the City in the event of Brexit. One is the majority view that global companies, which chose London partly because it is the world's largest trading centre for the euro with access to the Single Market, would relocate much of their operation inside the EU. The other is that we have heard all this before at the launch of the euro in 2000, when there was a lot of paranoia fuelled by claims that the new currency would mean the demise of the City. It proved to be far from the case, with twice as many euros traded in London in 2012 as in the whole of the rest of the eurozone. One senior City figure said:

It is possible that London, being outside the EU, could still survive as an offshore financial centre in the way that Singapore is a major centre or Hong Kong outside mainstream China. It is not clear if being outside would be the death knell for London, but it would certainly not be as beneficial as being on the inside.

There are undoubtedly parts of the EU system, including many MEPs and some member states, which are hostile to the 'Anglo-Saxon model' of capitalism or want to claim back some of the euro business conducted in the City. A European Central Bank policy paper in 2011 demanded that clearing houses, another key part of City life, should be based in the eurozone if they handle more than 5 per cent of the market in a euro-denominated financial product. The British government immediately took the ECB to the European Court of Justice to protect the City. Otherwise the ECB demands would force a partial relocation away from the City of LCH. Clearnet, one of the world's largest clearing houses, which processes most of the share trading on the London Stock Exchange and operates a derivatives clearing service. Big European banks that employ hundreds of staff in London are also likely to come under pressure to quit London whether or not the UK leaves the EU. That is because companies like Deutsche Bank and BNP Paribas have their main wholesale activities for products like derivatives in London while using their retail branches in Europe to underwrite this. The proposed new supervisor at the ECB, based in Frankfurt, could well insist that the entire operation is carried out under the jurisdiction of the planned eurozone Banking Union, forcing them to relocate away from the City. It would be another challenge to the dominance of the City that could be met with action in the European Court of Justice on the grounds of fair competition in the EU – not a legal avenue open to Britain on the outside.

There are two powerful reasons for the City staying inside both the Single Market and the EU. One is the familiar argument that Britain will lose a voice at the table when making the rules, even if it followed Norway into the European Economic Area in order to stay inside the Single Market. Britain still rarely gets outvoted on financial services issues – the first time in forty years of membership was in March 2013 when George Osborne, the Chancellor, failed in his attempt to block an EU cap on bankers' bonuses of twice annual salary. The other argument is that only an EU or EEA member state can provide the financial services 'passport' necessary for companies based in that country to do business in every other EU country. Large international banks, including from non-Single Market member Switzerland, base themselves in the City of London for this reason. Without this ability, London-based banks and other organisations from the US, China and Japan would need to relocate to another member state to get the passport to do business in the EU nations. If the UK was not in the Single Market, British banks or insurance firms or hedge funds would need a passport from another EU country, which would mean a sizeable presence would probably be required in that country.

TheCityUK, an independent body that represents the financial sector, analysed the sources of the £61 billion tax take from the financial services industry in 2008–09 and identified three main groups in terms of who might stay or go if Britain quit the EU. The largest group was of domestic financial services providers, generating £35–41 billion in tax, who would find it 'hard to impossible to leave' the UK; the second group was 'sticky but not unmovable', mostly major international banks which contributed £17–22 billion in tax; the third category with 'lowest hurdles to departure' consisted of highly paid foreign nationals and international finance firms headquartered in the City out of convenience, contributing £3 billion. 'We found that the internationally mobile cohort accounts for up to £25 billion of the tax take to the Treasury,' said Chris Cummings, CEO of TheCityUK.

> The reason why these firms stay is not because of the domestic market of 63 million but because they want access to the European market of 440 million. Once an institution from the US, China or Japan decide they want to be in Europe the question is, where is the best place to be based. That comes down to a fight between Paris, Frankfurt and London. The time zone, language, skills base and cluster factor of all these firms here benefit the City.

TheCityUK believes Britain is better off staying inside the Single Market for financial services and this is 'nothing to do with politics, simply the money'.

The British Bankers' Association has called for the government to get more involved in the EU to steer legislation. It believes that the benefits of EU membership outweigh the annoyances of regulation. 'The Single Market in financial services has been an essential ingredient in the creation of the global financial centre which London now is,' said Anthony Browne, chief executive of the BBA.

> For a lot of businesses in the City, it [leaving the EU] would be utterly devastating. It depends what 'out' looks

like. If we end up still being part of the Single Market and somehow contributing to the rules of the Single Market while not being a member then it does not really matter. But if you stop being part of the Single Market and lose the ability to 'passport' activities then it will make it very difficult for a lot of the businesses operating in the City to deliver their services to customers across Europe. They would have to apply for reauthorisation in an EU country. The political reality is if the UK left then I am sure there would be so much political momentum particularly in France and Germany to put up barriers to London businesses selling their services across Europe. I just cannot see that they would tolerate all the financial services business going to London.

Citigroup, the huge US bank, issued its own warning in 2013 that there was 'mounting concern' among its clients about their ability to continue using the UK as a regional hub if it left the EU. Another US giant, Goldman Sachs, went further, warning that it would 'drastically reduce' its activities in London and move large numbers of jobs to Germany and France if Britain left the European Union. The American bank uses London as its European main hub, employing 5,500 people at Fleet Street compared with 200 in Frankfurt and 100 in Paris. Michael Sherwood, the bank's co-chief executive in Europe, said: 'In all likelihood we would transfer a substantial part of our European business from London to a eurozone location – the most obvious contenders being Paris and Frankfurt.' In the event of Brexit, Dublin is also seen as a potential destination for other City firms like asset managers with large portfolios in the EU that want to retain the benefits of timezone and language. Leaving the EU and its Single Market will probably diminish the role of the City and reduce its earning power for the UK, at least in the short to medium term – and could even lead to a rebalancing of the British economy away from its reliance on financial services.

DEFENCE AND SECURITY

IN British Armed Forces take part in missions organised under the EU Common Security and Defence Policy such as Atalanta to protect ships from Somalian pirates. A British ambassador attends the twice-weekly Political and Security Committee meetings in Brussels. The UK strongly resists the creation of an EU military operations HQ or an EU army.

OUT Britain can build on its strong military cooperation with France, the only other major armed power in the EU, and coordinate with European allies through NATO. UK post-war security has always been based on NATO and the 'Five Eyes' pact to share intelligence with the US, Canada, Australia and New Zealand.

KEY STATS EU nations have more military personnel than the US and are second only to China with 5.4 million active or reserve forces. The UK and France make up half the military capacity of all EU states and carry out 70 per cent of the EU spending on military research and development. At 2.5 per cent of GDP in 2012, UK military spending is the largest in the EU; the US spends 4.4 per cent of GDP.

In one of the most embarrassing security breaches of the post-war era, it was revealed in 2013 that the Chancellor of Germany's private phone had been bugged for many years by foreign agents. The spies were not from an enemy power, however, but from the United States of America, one of Germany's key international allies. Details emerged from the whistle-blower Edward Snowden just days after President Obama had been welcomed in Berlin by Angela Merkel for private

discussions and a speech in front of the Brandenburg
Gate. Obama's visit was timed to commemorate the
fiftieth anniversary of President Kennedy's historic visit
to West Berlin when he memorably declared himself at
one with the German struggle for freedom. As a symbol
of close friendship, the US had been allowed to build
its embassy right next door to the historic columned
gateway in the heart of Berlin, just a stone's throw
from the new Chancellery building. A secret listening
post on top of that embassy was allegedly involved in
eavesdropping on Merkel's calls on behalf of the US
National Security Agency (NSA). At an EU summit in
October 2013 to discuss Snowden's disclosure that the
NSA routinely captured data on millions of phone calls
and emails across Europe, not to mention Mrs Merkel's
private conversations and possibly those of the Italian
Prime Minister too, David Cameron was strangely
taciturn as a joint statement was agreed. 'Cameron was
present at the discussion. He listened to it. He wasn't
against it. That is silent acquiescence as far as I go,' was
how Merkel described the British Prime Minister's clear
discomfort. The next day, *L'Espresso* newspaper claimed
that British intelligence cooperated with the Americans
to spy on the Italian government. Cameron refused to
respond to allegations that GCHQ assisted in NSA
surveillance and signed a statement from all twenty-
eight leaders acknowledging 'deep concerns among
European citizens' at the NSA revelations, warning that
'a lack of trust could prejudice the necessary cooperation
in the field of intelligence gathering'. The British Prime

Minister left the summit having secured one of his key aims – to delay new EU Data Protection Rules agreed by the European Parliament which would impose fines of up to €100 million on companies such as Facebook or Google if they broke rules on safeguarding personal data. 'The UK wanted to delay the Data Protection Rules because they feel that they may harm the interests of business,' Merkel explained after the summit.

A clear faultline had been dramatically exposed in Europe's security cooperation by the Snowden leaks which had actually been there all along. Britain and the US signed a top secret deal to share intelligence material in 1946, later joined by Canada, Australia and New Zealand – the English-speaking Second World War allies. The existence of the agreement, informally known as 'Five Eyes' after the classification 'AUS/CAN/NZ/UK/US EYES ONLY', was not publicly known until 2005. The response of Germany to discovering that some of its closest allies were listening in to its people and its politicians was to ignore MEPs who wanted to suspend trade talks between the US and EU and put out feelers on becoming the sixth 'eye'. There was little chance of that. Not only was the US historically reluctant to extend the club beyond the key nations of the so-called Anglosphere, Germany was historically reluctant to take part in the more aggressive 'defence' operations underpinned by the Five Eyes network, most notably the Iraq invasion of 2003 which split the EU down the middle. Britain's commitment to a common EU defence and security programme was called into question across the continent. 'The UK's leaders take pride in its partnership with the US and its membership of the Five Eyes Pact. And, by most accounts, it does so with the substantial support of its citizens. This begs the question: how European is Britain?' wrote Juliane Mendelsohn, a lecturer in European law at Berlin's Free University, in *The European* magazine. Thorsten Benner, director of the Global Public Policy Institute (GPPi) in Berlin, added: 'There is no united Europe when it comes to surveillance. A chief enemy of privacy rights is part of the European Union: the government of the United Kingdom ... As the Snowden documents reveal, the NSA even pays the UK to operate as the European hub for surveillance.'

For many years after it joined the European club, Britain was firmly against extending the EU's remit to include a common defence policy. That was what NATO was for, the military alliance also based in Brussels that guarded Europe throughout the Cold War. In 1998, there was a sudden change of policy. Tony Blair, anxious to place Britain as 'one of the leading countries of Europe' but unable to join the euro because of Gordon Brown's opposition, made an announcement after talks at St Malo with Jacques Chirac, leader of the EU's other nuclear military power.

The European Union needs to be in a position to play its full role on the international stage ... This includes the responsibility of the European Council to decide on the progressive framing of a common defence policy in the framework of Common Foreign and Security Policy. The Union must have the capacity for autonomous action, backed up by credible military forces, the means to decide to use them and a readiness to do so, in order to respond to international crises. In order for the European Union to take decisions and approve military action where the Alliance [NATO] as a whole is not engaged, the Union must be given appropriate structures and a capacity for analysis of situations, sources of intelligence and a capability for relevant strategic planning, without unnecessary duplication.

The humanitarian, rescue and peace-keeping responsibilities of the Western European Union, a Cold War alliance dating back to 1954, were moved to the EU and a Common Security and Defence Policy developed. Blair agreed to the creation of eighteen joint EU battlegroups and, since 2007, two units of 1,500 troops are on constant standby. The units were seen as a prototype for the European Army that has long been the dream of integrationists, who believe that the EU cannot emerge as a true global power by the use of 'soft power' alone. Viviane Reding, Luxembourg's member of the European Commission, tweeted in 2013 that: 'A European Army would be more efficient and would bring savings of between three and nine billion euros a year.' The December 2013 EU summit showed once again, however, that just as with intelligence security, the UK remained firmly against moving to the next level on European defence. Cameron objected to a plan for the

European Commission to have a stake in a 'European generation' of drones capable of flying for twenty-four hours, to be ready by 2020 for deployment at border crossing points and disaster areas. British diplomats purged the final communiqué of references to 'Europe's Armed Forces' and added clarification that defence policy should be left up to individual member states. Britain continued to resist calls for a permanent EU operational military headquarters, as it has done since this was first formally proposed in 2003 by France, Germany, Belgium and Luxembourg. 'What the EU does should be focused on practical action, facilitating what member states may want or choose to do together,' a Downing Street source told *The Times*. 'Take drones as an example. There can be no question of the Commission owning dual use military capabilities such as drones. Defence kit must be nationally owned and controlled and that should be clear to everyone.' A French call for an EU fund to help cover the costs of unilateral missions such as its armed intervention in Central African Republic was also shot down, this time by Germany.

Despite the obvious disagreements between Europe's major powers over defence and security coordination, there are those who believe that Britain has a lot to lose in this area by pulling out of the EU. Some analysts foresee a vacuum developing as the US tires of performing most of the heavy lifting for NATO to resolve problems in Europe's backyard while EU member states keep failing to step up to the mark. US impatience with Europe's continued weak military cooperation began with the wars triggered by the break-up of Yugoslavia. The Foreign Minister of Luxembourg, Jacques Poos, declared in 1991 that 'the hour of Europe has dawned' as he arrived to broker a peace treaty in Slovenia. In the wider context of the Balkans, however, he could not have been more wrong and Europe's disastrous inability to prevent or resolve the Bosnian and Kosovan wars in the 1990s left NATO with the responsibility of ending conflicts in which more than 100,000 died and two million were displaced. Fast-forward twenty years and Libya, another of Europe's neighbours, erupted into civil war. Once again there was EU political disagreement, with the spectacle at a Brussels summit in March 2011 of the EU High Representative for Foreign Affairs, Baroness Ashton, joining Germany in opposing the call from Britain and France for a no-fly zone to protect civilians. Thanks to a UN Security Council resolution just six days later in favour of a no-fly zone, the French and British began to enforce it the following week supported by the Americans in a mission soon taken over by NATO. If President Obama's 'pivot' towards Asia was not a clear enough sign that the US was beginning to move on from fighting Europe's battles, Robert Gates, the US Defense Secretary, gave notice in a speech in Brussels in 2011 of a 'dim if not dismal future' for NATO unless the Europeans started to pull their weight. 'For most of the Cold War US governments could justify defence investments and costly forward bases that made up roughly 50 per cent of all NATO military spending,' Gates said.

But some two decades after the collapse of the Berlin Wall, the US share of NATO defence spending has now risen to more than 75 per cent – at a time when politically painful budget and benefit cuts are being considered at home. The blunt reality is that there will be dwindling appetite and patience in the US Congress – and in the American body politic writ large – to expend increasingly precious funds on behalf of nations that are apparently unwilling to devote the necessary resources or make the necessary changes to be serious and capable partners in their own defence ... Indeed, if current trends in the decline of European defence capabilities are not halted and reversed, future US political leaders – those for whom the Cold War was *not* the formative experience that it was for me – may not consider the return on America's investment in NATO worth the cost.

With declining levels of national defence spending as a result of the financial crisis, the EU will have no choice but to develop its common defence and security system if its member states continue to neglect NATO and the US scales back its involvement. That means Britain, if it leaves the EU, could find itself left on the outside, or at best taking part as an associate rather than a full member. An independent Britain would not have the same considerable control over the levers of EU defence and security as it does now thanks to its military spending and expertise, some argue. In an essay for Regent's University, Jolyon Howorth, Jean Monnet Professor of European Studies at Bath University, said:

The bottom line is that there is a very clear time-limit on the willingness of Americans to continue to supply global public goods to European allies who are both wealthier and more numerous than they are, who face no existential threat, and who appear to be doing all too little to contribute to their own regional stability... Could the EU develop a robust security and defence capacity without the UK? The answer comes in two parts.

The first is that Common Security and Defence Policy (CSDP) without the UK would be a pale shadow of what it might be if the UK were fully involved. The second is that, because the European defence and security project arises out of the movement of history's tectonic plates, CSDP would have no alternative but to continue to develop, even without the UK. By the same token, the UK, because it is a significant defence player geographically situated in Europe, would have no alternative but to continue to have some sort of relationship with CSDP. This might involve the negotiation of a special status for the UK (similar to that of Turkey perhaps) within the European security project. But whatever the precise nature of such an arrangement, the UK would clearly henceforth wield significantly less clout in CSDP than it has to date ... The absence of the UK will undoubtedly lead to ever closer security and defence cooperation between France and Germany (however fraught with problems programmatically and strategically), and, beyond that, with the Weimar group (France, Germany and Poland) supplemented by Italy and Spain. It would be very difficult for France to find a justification for establishing a privileged partnership with a 'post-Brexit' UK which looked fixedly across the Atlantic rather than across the Channel.

France, however, is fully aware that Brexit is a possibility and nevertheless seems to have concluded that it stands a better chance of remaining an important military actor in a bilateral partnership with the UK than under the EU's patchy CSDP. In 2013, after France intervened (backed up by British non-combat support) in Mali following a coup , Colonel Michel Goya, a teacher at the Institut de Recherche Strategique de l'Ecole Militaire in Paris, told the EUobserver website that, 'If you have to react quickly to events, it is better to do it at a national or bi-national level.' In other words, the EU was just too cumbersome to deliver a meaningful military response. France and the UK signed a Treaty on Defence and Security Co-operation in November 2010. The areas of cooperation include aircraft carriers, transport aircraft, nuclear submarines, military satellite technology, drones, expeditionary forces and eventually combat systems. The two countries are indisputably the EU's leading military powers, spending €92 billion on defence in 2012, more than Germany, Italy, the Netherlands, Poland and Spain put together. 'As shown from our joint operations in Libya and Mali, the UK and France are natural partners and have a key role to play in leading and shaping the defence and security of Europe,' a British Defence Ministry spokesman said in September 2012. The British and French army, navy and air force regularly train together and British officers serve full time on the French aircraft carrier, the *Charles de Gaulle*. They are on track to create a Combined Joint Expeditionary Force (CJEF) by 2016 and are building a 'Future Combat Air System' due in 2030. In Britain, successive Conservative Defence Secretaries have been among the most eurosceptic Cabinet members. Liam Fox, who held the post from 2010 to 2011, said in January 2013 that, 'If the choice for me was between going in the current direction – which, let's face it, is towards ever closer union and ultimately a greater and greater loss of British sovereignty – then my personal preference would be to leave.' His successor Philip Hammond said in May 2013 that he wanted a renegotiated membership deal but without that he could contemplate leaving. The deepening military cooperation with France led by these two politicians looks like the foundation of a post-EU defence strategy for Britain.

EDUCATION, RESEARCH
AND SCIENCE

IN British academics win a disproportionately high number of grants from the European Research Council (18.7 per cent) but British students take a disproportionately low number of placements at European universities on the Erasmus exchange scheme (5.4 per cent).

OUT The UK could still take part in the EU's research programme and Erasmus student exchange scheme, provided the other member states agreed and it paid to take part like Norway and Switzerland.

KEY STATS British-based researchers won €6.1 billion of the €50.5 billion available in the 2007–13 EU research programme (12 per cent), including €1.4 billion out of €7.5 billion of grants from the European Research Council.[45] There were 132,555 EU students at UK universities in 2011–12, up 1.9 per cent on the previous academic year and 5.3 per cent of the total.[46]

After gaining his PhD in metal physics, Andre Geim spurned his native Russia to work in the US, UK and Netherlands before deciding that Britain was the best place to be based as an academic researcher. His initial notoriety came from discovering a magnetic technique with water which he demonstrated by levitating a frog. Then he published an academic paper in the name of his favourite hamster. As a professor at Manchester University, Geim and fellow Russian émigré Konstantin Novoselov discovered the ultra-thin material graphene in 2004 while funded by Britain's Engineering and Physical Sciences Research Council (EPSRC). Geim and Novoselov used a sophisticated form of sticky tape to strip graphite down to the atomic level. At just one molecule thick, graphene is a million times thinner than a sheet of paper but 200 times stronger than steel. 'We devote 10 per cent of our time to so-called "Friday evening" experiments,' said Novoselov. 'I just do all kinds of crazy things that probably won't pan out, but if they do ... This graphene business started as a Friday evening experiment.' Novoselov won an EU-funded grant of €1.78 million from the European Research Council in 2007 while Geim and his team picked up another £5 million from EPSRC in 2009 to work on the potential of graphene, which has been hailed as the wonder material of the twenty-first century, with the potential to replace silicon in computing among many other possible uses from 'wearable electronics' to stronger condoms. The pair was awarded the Nobel Prize for Physics in 2010. It was a big moment for the EPSRC but also for the European Research Council – Novoselov was the first Nobel laureate in its short history following its creation by the EU in 2007. The British government acted to try and ensure that graphene development stayed in the UK with grants of £21.5 million awarded in 2012 through the EPSRC to six universities, including Manchester where the National Graphene Institute is being built with £38 million of government money and £23 million of EU regional development funding. Geim and Novoselov, who both hold joint citizenship, were knighted in the New Year's Honours List 2012. The EU went even further in 2013, announcing the 'Graphene Flagship' deal – a ten-year research programme for 126 academic and industrial research groups in seventeen European countries to be funded by €1 billion from the EU budget. While Britain will clearly have to fight to stay at the forefront of a material discovered at a British university, the Graphene Flagship is one answer to those who ask whether the EU ever spends taxpayers' cash on forward-looking European innovation.

The EU's overall budget agreement for the seven-year period from 2014 to 2020 saw the first real terms cut in spending – by 3.7 per cent – following calls for restraint led by the British government. Research was one of the few policy areas to be handed an increase. Spending will rise by 52.5 per cent to €77 billion from €50.5 billion in 2007–13, with the European Research Council receiving €13.1 billion of that, up from €7.5 billion. British universities and researchers do relatively well in competition for EU grants with other countries and are second only to their counterparts in Germany in accessing EU research funding, winning €6.1 billion of the 2007–13 budget. At around 12 per cent of the funds available, this proportion was roughly equal to Britain's contribution to the overall EU budget. It has become an invaluable source of funding for several UK universities, accounting for at least 10 per cent of their research income and helping to attract and keep top academics in the UK. Cambridge ranked fourth among all participants worldwide in the seven-year research programme from 2007 to 2013 with more than €370 million in grants, closely followed by Oxford with just under €370 million. The top ten also included University College London in seventh with €309 million and Imperial College London (ninth with €296 million). British businesses also received a slice of the cake with 2,800 firms sharing €800 million, with Rolls-Royce awarded €20 million in research cash. If Britain left the EU, it could pay to stay in the EU's research programme as non-EU member Switzerland did in the 2007–13 programme, signing an agreement to contribute €1.4 billion or 3 per cent of the budget. Its researchers received around €1.8 billion in funding. Swiss involvement had to be approved by other member states, which could present problems for Britain given its disproportionate success rate at winning grants. But why would an independent UK pay to join an EU programme rather than simply commit the same level of funds to its own universities and companies? Most EU grants are given to consortia of researchers from several countries and only by full participation can a country lead one of these projects. It is possible to join in by invitation – and researchers from the US and around the world join consortia receiving EU funds – but the lead researcher must be based in a member state. Plus Britain would lose its role at the table when deciding on research strategy, such as the choice of graphene for one of two flagship projects chosen from twenty-three proposals.

At undergraduate level, growing numbers of universities across the EU are introducing courses in English to attract British students deterred by the steep rise in domestic course fees (except for Scottish students in Scotland) of up to £9,000 a year. Universities in Denmark and Sweden do not charge undergraduates for tuition while those in the Netherlands have a much lower fee, with the University of Maastricht staging a recruitment drive for British students for courses priced at €1,906 for the 2014/15 academic year. The impact of the higher rate of British course fees on student mobility has yet to be fully felt, with OECD figures dating from 2009 showing only 22,000 UK students studying full-time in the EU (as opposed to spending just a year abroad as part of a UK-based course), a figure which has the potential to rise sharply. The numbers of EU students in British institutions has been rising, from 125,045 in the 2009/10 academic year to 132,555 in 2011/12, the last year of lower fees, so the full impact of the £9,000 fee is not yet clear on EU student numbers. Since Britain imports many more students from the EU than it exports, eurosceptics argue that there would be a large net income gain if UK institutions were able to charge full international fees. With classroom-based degrees generally costing one third more for non-EU students and medical courses three times as much, there could be a considerable windfall for UK universities in the event of British EU withdrawal – provided that the higher fees did not in turn put the EU students off. EU countries would also then apply international rates to British students, reducing their appeal, although in many cases they would still be cheaper – Maastricht University's tuition fee for non-EU students is €8,500 a year for arts and €9,500 for science.

The EU's level playing field for undergraduate fees also means that EU students can access government-subsidised support from the Student Loan Company. But the recovery of these loans is causing growing concern. By the end of the 2012/13 financial year, the amount of money lent to European students was £484.5 million, with £184.4 million of this liable for repayment and £11.4 million classed as in arrears. The SLC announced in 2013 that it had hired private investigators to track down those evading payment in Europe. Loans for tuition costs would no longer have to be provided from the SLC to EU students if the UK withdrew from the Union.

One of the main pan-European higher education projects is the Bologna Process, founded in 1998 by the UK, France, Germany and Italy, to harmonise and integrate university processes and standards. This has been joined by forty-seven countries in the European Higher Education Area and, although EU member states lead the way, would remain open to the UK outside the EU. Cooperation and collaboration between scholars has been a feature of European higher education for centuries and will continue whether Britain is in or out of the EU. And despite fears to the contrary, a British departure from the EU need not bring an end to Erasmus, a popular scheme for student and staff placements in European universities. Erasmus provides grants for undergraduate placements of three to twelve months. Around 200,000

British students have been abroad on the Erasmus programme since it began in 1987, with 13,662 receiving an average monthly allowance of just under €400 each from the EU in 2011/12. British universities receive around twice as many students as they send to Europe, a total of 25,760 in 2011/12. Erasmus was another of the few areas to receive a rise in the 2014–20 EU budget, going up by 40 per cent to €14.7 billion and extending the beneficiaries to include 'youth leaders, volunteers and young sportsmen'. This led some anti-EU MEPs to question why more cash should be spent on non-means-tested grants to university students while other initiatives are being cut. Stuart Agnew, a UKIP MEP, told the European Parliament:

Erasmus is simply a glorified student exchange programme which we could do without the existence of the EU. UK universities have numerous exchange programmes all over the world without needing to be in a political union. Erasmus is not really about educational excellence, is it? It is to cynically use young people to further your political aims.

Mairead McGuinness, an Irish Fine Gael MEP, asked Agnew if he had 'any respect for young people and their ability to discern what is right and what is wrong and their ability as mature young people to live and to learn by sharing experience'. Agnew replied: 'I am not insulting youth at all. What really worries me is the way they are being used by the European Union to further its own objectives. Throw money at young people, tell them how wonderful the EU is and they will vote for it.' Several non-EU countries, however, including Turkey and Switzerland, have already joined Erasmus by paying a membership fee, so Britain could continue its involvement in the scheme should it leave the EU and provided that the member states accept an application to take part.

ENVIRONMENT, CLIMATE CHANGE AND ENERGY

IN Britain must close 11GW of high-emission power plants by 2015. The Reach Directive of 2006 imposes bureaucratic requirements on industry to test and register the chemicals they use. Britain must reuse or recycle 50 per cent of household waste by 2020 under the Waste Framework Directive.

OUT Britain could scale back its ambitious renewable energy target and exempt manufacturers (but not exporters to the EU) from the Reach Directive. A number of United Nations protocols demand strict environmental controls even if Britain found itself outside the EU.

KEY STATS The European Commission is proposing a new binding target of 40 per cent lower greenhouse gas emissions than 1990 by 2030, while the UK has already set a national target of 50 per cent less by 2025. The UK is struggling to meet its EU target of 15 per cent of renewable energy by 2020. UK greenhouse gas emissions rose 3.2 per cent from 2011 to 2012.[47]

Two small earthquakes hit the Lancashire coast in 2011 and signalled a new phase in the battle over a controversial technique for retrieving huge amounts of gas trapped deep under half the land mass of the UK. The tremors led to a temporary ban on the controversial technique of fracking – short for hydraulic fracturing – the practice of releasing gas from shale rock layers by blasting them with high pressure water and chemicals.

An independent report commissioned by the energy company Cuadrilla conceded it was 'highly probable' that the tremors were caused by its test drilling but added that earthquakes were 'unlikely to occur again' because of the 'unusual combination of geology' at the site. By December 2012, the government had lifted the national fracking ban but the European Commission was looking into the environmental implications of exploiting the potentially vast amount of gas lying underneath many EU countries. In Britain alone, reserves are said to be sufficient to supply the country with gas for at least fifty years, although experts caution that only a fraction could possibly be extracted. Still, after fracking transformed the energy debate in the United States by dramatically cutting both prices and greenhouse gas emissions, it is a huge temptation for politicians in Europe at a time of public disquiet over rising energy prices and an increasing reliance on gas and coal from Russia.

The EU already has an array of regulations to protect the environment from the potentially harmful side effects of fracking, such as ground water pollution controls and strict rules on greenhouse gas releases. So while France introduced a ban on the technique and Germany a moratorium, the UK government teamed up with Poland, the EU country with the largest gas reserves and fewest qualms about exploiting them, to put pressure on the bureaucrats in Brussels not to add to the legal constraints. 'It is essential the EU minimise the regulatory burdens and costs on industry and domestic bill payers by not creating uncertainty or introducing new legislation,' David Cameron wrote to José Manuel Barroso, the European Commission President, in December 2013. 'The industry in the UK has told us that new EU legislation would delay imminent investment.' In a leaked letter, Ivan Rogers, Britain's ambassador to the EU, warned that even if successful in avoiding the threat of legislation 'we will need a longer term strategy to manage the risks including ... an influencing strategy for the new European Parliament and Commission'. In January 2014, the European Commission decided against new laws on fracking although it said it would monitor drilling closely and review the situation in eighteen months. In a long-awaited announcement on its future environmental goals, the Commission also backed away from further tough national targets on renewable energy, recognising that some countries favoured nuclear energy and fracking as important parts of their energy mix. The British government's successful lobbying effort won an instant vote of confidence from French energy company Total which, shut out of its home market, announced investment of up to £30 million in test drilling in Lincolnshire. It also won admiring headlines, including the *Daily Mail*'s 'EU scraps targets forcing Britain to build wind farms: UK free to go nuclear and use fracking'. While the EU does not force wind farms on member states – it is their choice how to meet renewable targets – this reflected how Brussels has an important influence over environmental and energy choices. The question is whether the UK would be free and willing to make different choices following a vote to leave the Union.

Environmental legislation made in Brussels has long been a target of eurosceptics for criticism and potential repatriation to UK control. 'We need to examine whether the balance is right in so many areas where the European Union has legislated including on the environment, social affairs and crime. Nothing should be off the table,' Cameron said in his Bloomberg speech. In Open Europe's list of the most expensive EU regulations according to the government's own assessment studies, four of the top ten concern the environment, including the Climate and Energy Package of 2009 costing £3.36 billion a year and the Building and Approved Inspectors (Amendment) Regulations 2006 and the Energy Performance of Buildings (Certificates and Inspectors) (England and Wales) Regulations 2007 costing £1.5 billion a year. As seen in the Prosperity chapter, the government claimed a ludicrous level of potential benefits from the Climate and Energy Package when it was agreed in 2009. Instead, the costs have been huge. The package includes the Renewables Directive, the Emissions Trading Directive and the Directive on the Geological Storage of Carbon Dioxide – some of the most expensive and criticised of all the EU's attempts to give a global lead on environmental protection.

The Renewables Directive for the first time dictated to EU member states the make-up of their national energy mix. While not ordering any particular method, it brought in an EU target for 20 per cent of energy to come from renewable sources by 2020 across the member states, with Britain's share to rise from 1.3 per cent in 2005 to 15 per cent (the biggest leap of any country). UK ministers believed that incentives to make such a dramatic increase in wind, wave, biomass or solar power would flow from emissions trading, an experiment which Britain began in 2002 ahead of the EU's own Emissions Trading Scheme (ETS) at a time when the UK was keen to be seen as a world leader in green economics. It didn't work out as planned. The ETS has been a shambles because the EU handed out far too many permits. It reckoned without a fall in demand for energy caused by the recession which saw the price of permits crash from nearly €30 each in 2008 to a low of less than €3 in January 2013. Emissions actually rose by 1.9 per cent during the first phase of the EU trading scheme and by 5.8 per cent in the UK. From 2011 to 2012 EU emissions went up by 2.4 per cent and UK emissions by 3.2 per cent. The UK responded by introducing a floor price in its permits of £16 per tonne of CO_2, going much further than the EU dared to go in adding costs to industry – and to consumers. While the EU moved in late 2013 to delay issuing a large quantity of permits in an attempt to drive the prices back up, analysts predict it will still be years before they rise above the €20 level deemed necessary to prompt industry and utilities to make a fundamental shift to green energy.

The failure to inspire a sufficient increase in sustainable energy production has meant that another EU

directive designed to remove high-emitting facilities
is in danger of being overtaken by events. The Large
Combustion Plant Directive of 2001 will see 11GW of
UK generating capacity closed down by the end of 2015.
It has become a target for eurosceptic campaigners, with
the Fresh Start group of Conservative MPs warning that:

> The UK currently has around 97GW of generation
> capacity covering an estimated peak demand of 57.1GW.
> However, of this only 64.1GW of generation capacity
> is 'base load' or reliable for peak periods, this currently
> gives the UK a spare peak time capacity of 13 per cent.
> However, as a result of the removal of large plants from
> production the base load is predicted to fall to 46.8 GW.
> Unless measures are taken, this could leave the UK with
> very little or no peak time generation cover, potentially
> leading to blackouts.

The problem could be compounded by Britain's slow
response to replacing its ageing nuclear energy capacity,
with the planned closure of 7GW of nuclear generation
by 2020. The first new atomic plant commissioned by
the UK government this century is not due to come on
line until 2023 at Hinkley Point in Somerset. But the
contract with French provider EDF has come under
investigation from another arm of the EU machine – its
competition directorate. That is because the government
agreed to guarantee the price paid for the nuclear energy
for thirty-five years, whatever the market rate. 'The
European Commission needs to investigate thoroughly

its impact on the UK and the EU internal energy markets,' said Joaquin Almunia, the Competition Commissioner. Ministers dismissed the inquiry as a formality – but a dangerous one as they are counting on Hinkley Point to provide 7 per cent of the UK's electricity at full capacity. Meanwhile, Ofgem, the electricity and gas regulator, warned in 2013 of an increased risk of power blackouts because spare capacity in 2015 will be limited to just 2 per cent, a level at which the National Grid might have to intervene to tell industry to cut back on usage.

It is tempting to blame the EU for causing Britain's looming energy crunch by a mixture of ambitious greenhouse gas targets, the forced closure of coal-fired power stations and a failed investment strategy due partly to the problems of the Emissions Trading Scheme. But the UK has actually been running ahead of Brussels on most of these environmentally inspired measures. Britain's transition to low-carbon energy began in 2000 with a Royal Commission on Environmental Pollution that recommended a cut in emissions by 60 per cent below 1990 levels by 2050. Then Ed Miliband, as Energy and Climate Change Secretary, announced that the 2008 Climate Change Act would require the government to cut emissions by 80 per cent by 2050 in the toughest target set by any country in the world. In May 2011, Chris Huhne, then Energy and Climate Secretary, committed the UK to making 50 per cent emissions cuts by 2025. Successive British governments have imposed strict environmental targets on themselves.

Outside the EU, Britain could revise its renewable

energy target of 15 per cent by 2020, although it was content to sign up to this under the Labour government in 2009. It could repeal the regulations that implemented the Large Combustion Plant Directive but a policy u-turn back to higher emissions from coal-fired power stations would face stiff opposition on environmental grounds – even with cheap coal becoming available from the US as it steps up its gas production from fracking. And the UK could accelerate the controversial gas extraction technique, although it has been hampered far more by earthquakes in Lancashire than interference from Brussels. EU directives on water and air pollution will act as safeguards when fracking does begin in earnest and are unlikely to be repealed by an independent UK outside the EU.

One expensive directive that has hit industry hard is the Registration, Evaluation, Authorisation and Restriction of Chemicals (Reach) law of 2009 which requires companies to test and register with a new European Chemicals Agency every chemical compound used in their processes, above the level of one tonne per year. Although companies can share information, compliance costs have been estimated at €5 billion across the EU with a million more tests on animals required. Supporters say that it will more than pay for itself in savings in healthcare and environment costs. An independent UK could exempt manufacturers but not exporters of the onerous requirements. Reach's companion measure, the Classification, Labelling and Packaging (CLP) Regulation, which seeks to harmonise the way hazardous materials are classified and labelled, could not be similarly avoided, however, as it effectively implements the UN's Global Harmonized System for classifying hazardous substances. Similarly, many other EU environmental measures stem from international bodies. These include several important UN agreements such as the Gothenburg Protocol of 1999 setting limits for air pollutants; the Aarhus Convention of 2001 on public rights to environmental data; and the Kiev Protocol of 2010 on cross-border consultation on major projects with environmental impacts. Moreover there are signs of a slowdown in the EU's rush to be best in class for global environment lessons. The European Commission's proposed new target of 40 per cent lower emissions by 2030 is far less ambitious than the target agreed by the coalition government of 50 per cent by 2025. And following the announcement of a move from an overall 20 per cent EU renewable energy target by 2020 to 27 per cent by 2030, without binding individual country goals, environmental campaigners accused the European Commission of bowing to national pressure. 'The previously far-sighted and ambitious European Commission is a shadow of its former self, hiding behind the UK and other backward-looking member states and lobbies,' said Thomas Becker, CEO of the European Wind Energy Association. 'By effectively advocating repatriation of energy policy to member states, President Barroso appears to have forgotten his previous calls for "more European integration" on energy policy.' This was music to the ears of those campaigning for a return of environmental controls from Brussels to national capitals, and a boost for David Cameron's plans to negotiate a repatriation of powers ahead of a referendum on EU membership.

EMPLOYMENT AND
SOCIAL LAW

IN Employee protections brought in by the EU include four weeks' minimum paid annual leave, fourteen weeks' minimum maternity leave and four further months of possible childcare leave, equal treatment for agency workers and limits to working hours.

OUT Britain would be able to scrap expensive EU laws like the Working Time Directive but only if it left the Single Market. Small and medium-sized businesses could be exempted from expensive employee protections like equal treatment for agency workers.

KEY STATS The 100 most costly EU regulations are estimated to cost the UK economy £27.4 billion per year with the Working Time Directive alone said to cost £4.1 billion a year.[48]

In its founding treaty dating back to 1957, the forerunner of the European Union declared that one of its key aims was to 'promote improved working conditions and an improved standard of living for workers, so as to make possible their harmonisation' among the member states. Jacques Delors, the former French finance minister who was President of the European Commission from 1985 to 1994, made 'Social Europe' one of his top priorities. Delors, a Socialist who became the great nemesis of Britain's Conservative Prime Minister Margaret Thatcher, believed that the opening up of the Single Market should go hand-in-hand with the protection of workers' rights. He reasoned that unfettered competition could lead companies to relocate to cheaper areas or drive them to cut costs ruthlessly, leading to worsening workplace conditions, insecurity and job losses. 'The creation of a vast economic area, based on market and business cooperation, is inconceivable – I would say unattainable – without some harmonisation of social legislation. Our ultimate aim must be the creation of a European Social Area,' Delors said in 1986. The British government refused to sign up. The clash of ideologies helped to create the impression that a European superstate was being built by an alternative powerbase in Brussels. As mentioned in the Sovereignty chapter, Britain felt that the Working Time Directive and its provision for a maximum working week of forty-eight hours was brought in by the back door and that Britain was being bounced into a new era of involuntary European integration. 'The UK strongly opposes any attempt to tell people that they can no longer work the hours they want,' said David Hunt, the Employment Secretary.

The Working Time Directive would go on to have a big impact on British life and become emblematic of the 'red tape' from Brussels, even though the government has secured the possibility for individuals to opt out of its 48-hour working week. Nowhere was the impact of this directive more acutely felt than in the National Health Service, where the long hours culture of junior doctors in hospitals was already being tackled by a government

'New Deal' to bring in a 56-hour maximum working week. The Working Time Directive also provides for four weeks' paid holiday from work, a minimum rest period of eleven consecutive hours in every twenty-four and a minimum uninterrupted rest period of twenty-four hours every seven days. Its provisions were advanced by several rulings from the European Court of Justice, adding on-call time to working hours calculations even when the worker was having a sleep. As the Royal College of Physicians observed in a briefing paper in 2012, the Working Time Directive (WTD) played havoc with NHS training, rotas and consultant care. 'The training time for junior doctors with senior consultants has been reduced,' the Royal College wrote.

Application of WTD and the New Deal has resulted in more rota gaps, which are often left to junior doctors to fill. Therefore many trainee doctors are working much of their time at night and unsupervised, missing out on crucial learning opportunities with more senior colleagues. This may result in the need for prolongation of training for some individuals. This has significant potential implications for future patient care ... Similarly, there is insufficient out of hours consultant cover. This is particularly problematic for small district general hospitals providing acute services. A survey by the RCP in October 2010 found that only 3 per cent of hospitals provided weekend cover from consultant physicians specialising in acute medicine for nine to twelve hours and none for over twelve hours.

The bulk of the annual NHS bill for agency workers of £1 billion is for cover required due to the Working Time Directive and the total cost of the directive to the economy is estimated by Open Europe at £4.1 billion a year.

An estimated three million workers in Britain make use of the opt-out to work longer than forty-eight hours a week some or all of the time, from the hospitality industry to night porters, construction workers and contract labourers. The European Commission is keen to end the possibility of the individual opt-out but could only do so if a qualified majority of member states backed this in the European Council. So far, Britain is leading a blocking alliance – something it would not be able to do if it left the EU. If a post-referendum Britain joined the EEA, it would still have to apply the directive because it is deemed to be part of the Single Market. So if the European Commission got its way, a post-Brexit Britain in the EEA would also have to implement the 48-hour week with no opt-outs. In one example of the directive's far-reaching implications, Open Europe quoted David Dalziel, secretary of the Chief Fire Officers Association in Scotland, saying:

The potential loss of the individual opt-out in the UK would have catastrophic effects. Ninety-one per cent of the UK landmass is protected by firefighters on the retained duty system. These men and women crew two out of every three fire stations in the country. They hold other jobs in their local communities and also provide around 120 hours availability every week of the year to deliver a local fire and rescue service. Any adverse impact on that would expose this country to an unacceptable level of risk.

Open Europe has estimated the annual extra cost to employers of losing the opt-out at between £9.2 and £11.9 billion a year.

Labour and the Liberal Democrats have both spoken out against the way that the EU seeks to regulate employment through the Working Time Directive. But worker protections portrayed as bureaucratic and expensive by British business and politicians are viewed quite differently by the trade unions. In 2009, Brendan Barber, then General Secretary of the Trades Union Congress, said:

Long hours cause stress, illness and lower productivity. And when many employers are moving to short-time working, the need for an opt-out of the 48-hour week is even more out of date. The UK government still needs to tighten the law on working time, otherwise the EU could take it to court in order to protect UK workers from abuse of the 48-hour week.

Speaking at a TUC debate which voted overwhelmingly to end the British opt-out from the Working Time Directive, Tony Woodley, then joint leader of Britain's biggest union Unite, said: 'People don't want long hours. They work long hours because it is the only way to make ends meet. People should work to live – not live to work.' In 2013, Frances O'Grady, who replaced Barber as TUC General Secretary, said:

> Paid holidays and other workplace rights are some of
> the best arguments for EU membership. Leaving the
> EU would be disastrous for jobs and investment ... The
> Prime Minister wants to offer the dismal choice between
> leaving the EU or staying in a Europe stripped of rights
> at work.

After the Working Time Directive, the next most expensive directive on working conditions is thought to be the
Temporary Agency Workers Directive of 2008 which
brought extra annual costs estimated at £2 billion, according to Open Europe in 2013. The directive insists that
general working conditions for agency workers should be
the same as if they were recruited directly to the same
job by the same organisation. The government negotiated
with the Confederation of British Industry (CBI) and the
TUC for this requirement to come into effect once an
agency worker has completed twelve continuous calendar
weeks in the same role, at the same organisation. Like all
EU directives, it had to be brought in via UK law and was
implemented by the Agency Workers Regulations 2010.
The government's impact assessment estimated that
around 40 per cent of agency workers, around 520,000,
would be covered by the principle of equal treatment. It
also forecast that about 65,000 agency workers could
have their postings cut short to prevent them meeting the
twelve-week qualifying period for equal treatment. In a
survey of 200 medium-sized and large UK organisations
in 2011, one third of respondents said that they would
consider ending an agency workers' job before they had

served twelve weeks, in order to avoid the increased costs of equal treatment.

There are dozens of other EU social and employment laws, many concerned with technical aspects of health and safety, which the UK would wish to preserve even if it withdrew from Brussels. Ordinary workers have undoubtedly benefited, notably on maternity and paternity leave. The Pregnant Workers' Directive of 1992 established the basic right of a working mother to fourteen weeks off to give birth, as well as time off with protection from dismissal for ante-natal examinations. The Parental Leave Directive of 1996 brought a new right, included in the Employment Relations Act 1999, for every parent to take thirteen weeks unpaid leave to care for each child (in addition to maternity leave) before the child turns five years old. This was the kind of social provision from Brussels that Conservative governments had blocked, in this case since it was first proposed by the European Commission in 1983. The Parental Leave Directive of 1996 was then repealed by the EU in 2010 and replaced with a more far-reaching provision, enacted into British law in 2013 by Statutory Instrument No. 283, to extend unpaid parental leave from thirteen to eighteen weeks.

The Working Time Directive is clearly one of the Brussels laws that David Cameron has in his sights for renegotiation as part of the EU reform and repatriation of powers he envisages before holding a referendum on membership. In his 2012 speech to the Davos conference, he said:

In spite of the economic challenge, we are still doing things to make life even harder. In the name of social protection, the EU has promoted unnecessary measures that impose burdens on businesses and governments, and can destroy jobs. The Agency Workers Directive, the Pregnant Workers Directive, the Working Time Directive. The list goes on and on.

He returned to this theme at the 2014 Davos gathering:

Some in the European Commission seem to think that if they're not producing new regulations they're somehow not doing their job and that removing existing regulations is somehow an act of self-harm, while many in the European Parliament are tempted to gold-plate every piece of legislation. Let's be clear. We don't protect workers by piling on the regulations and directives to such an extent that they become unemployable. We have to maintain the flexibility for companies to grow and expand.

Cameron has been urged by the Fresh Start group to take back the powers conceded in 1997 when Tony Blair reversed John Major's position and agreed to sign up to the Social Chapter, giving the EU control over social and employment law. 'In the interests of economic competitiveness, member states should be able to determine their own mix of social and employment regulation, and the EU should reflect the principle of subsidiarity in this area,' the Fresh Start Mandate for Reform published in

November 2013 said. Subsidiarity is the EU principle that laws are framed at the level of government – local, national or supranational in Brussels – most appropriate to the subject matter. It rarely seems to work in the direction of national or local control, however. Such a return of powers to the national level over the whole field of employment and social legislation would require a change to the EU's treaties, something that requires unanimous agreement by all twenty-eight member states. Acknowledging this, the Fresh Start group called for interim measures to resist new EU laws:

> To ensure that excessive EU regulation does not strangle economic growth, the EU should apply a 'one in, one out' rule for all regulation, introduce sunset clauses (the time after which the regulation will expire, unless explicitly renewed) for all new regulations, and provide further exemptions for small and micro-businesses.

In his Bloomberg speech, Cameron showed that he wanted to try and take back powers over employment laws even if this meant attempting treaty change.

> We cannot harmonise everything. For example, it is neither right nor necessary to claim that the integrity of the single market or full membership of the European Union requires the working hours of British hospital doctors to be set in Brussels irrespective of the views of British parliamentarians and practitioners.

Other EU leaders have a different view – they believe that any such return of powers will unpick the necessary worker protections which go hand-in-hand with competition in the Single Market and lead to an unravelling of the entire EU project. Didier Reynders, the Belgian foreign minister, told Cameron in October 2013 that he wished to see the UK remain part of the EU but this could not mean 'à la carte' membership, echoing the warning to Britain in May 2012 from President Hollande of France, that 'Europe is not a cash till and less still a self-service restaurant'.

FARMING

IN British farmers belong to the same regime of subsidies and production standards as their European competitors, with UK ministers taking part in discussions to set the rules. Farmers are protected from global competition by common EU tariffs on imports.

OUT Britain would stop paying subsidies to European farmers while being free to modernise support payments to its own farmers and drop tariffs on imports to benefit consumers. Britain could import and grow genetically modified crops which are blocked in the EU by a group of member states led by France.

KEY STATS The Common Agricultural Policy took 39 per cent of EU spending, or €57 billion, in 2013. Nearly 200,000 British farmers share £3.3 billion a year from the EU, while £5.4 billion went to farming from the UK budget contribution in 2013, a net British subsidy to European farmers of £2.2 billion, or £6 million a day.[49]

At number eight on the 2013 *Sunday Times* Rich List with an estimated fortune of £7.8 billion, the 6th Duke of Westminster owed his great wealth to inherited land in some of the country's most desirable postcodes, including Mayfair and Belgravia in central London. His bank account is also boosted by a nice annual cheque from the European Union. His Grace's rural holdings received £748,716 through the Common Agricultural Policy (CAP) in 2011, according to information obtained from the Department for Environment, Food and Rural Affairs under Freedom of Information laws. He was not the only wealthy landowner helped by the taxpayer under the EU's oldest and most expensive system of subsidies. The Earl of Plymouth received £675,085, the Duke of Buccleuch £260,273, the Duke of Devonshire £251,729 and the Duke of Atholl £231,188. Brussels did not overlook the Windsor family. The Queen was given £415,817 for the Royal Farms and £314,811 for the Duchy of Lancaster, while Prince Charles was paid £127,868 for the Duchy of Cornwall.[50] An outcry over the amount of EU funds given to the extremely wealthy led to an attempt to limit annual payments under the CAP to €300,000 per owner. At the forefront of those opposing this move was the UK government, arguing that it would unfairly penalise British farmers for creating efficient, larger farms in contrast with the relatively uncompetitive smallholdings common in, say, France. 'The European Commission has this culture that small farms is how you do farming. We come from a completely different farming culture,' a British official said. Britain would have 330 farms losing money because of the proposed limit; France just thirty. In the end, the reform – like so many previous attempts to modernise the CAP – was watered down. In a compromise agreement, national governments must deduct at least 5 per cent from farm payments of more than €150,000 a year and can cut up to 100 per cent of the money above that level from 2015. The British government decided not to make any reductions to payments to wealthy landowners beyond the minimum 5 per cent. MPs on the Commons Select Committee for Environment, Food and

Rural Affairs called for a higher rate of reduction for farms receiving more than €300,000 a year. But Owen Paterson, the Secretary of State, explained that, 'I do not want to see our successful farmers spending hours and hours with expensive solicitors artificially carving up their holdings to avoid an arbitrary diktat on the size of their holding.' In other words, there was no point trying to reduce subsidies for rich landowners because they would only find a way to keep them. Between them, Brussels and Westminster seem incapable of finding a fairer way of funding farming.

Financial support for farmers has been a core European activity since the Common Agricultural Policy started in 1962. It was the price France demanded in return for agreeing to free trade in industrial goods. After the shortages and rationing of the post-war years, the aim was to ensure food security for Europe as well as to maintain the traditional farming practices which are so important for the rural economy, the landscape and the environment. Although the cost of the CAP reached 94 per cent of the EU budget in 1970, reform and the growing importance of regional funding slowly reduced that amount to 39 per cent by 2013, although it remains way out of kilter for a sector which employs 5 per cent of Europeans and contributes 1.7 per cent to the EU economy – and just 0.7 per cent in the UK. Subsidies have been de-coupled from production, avoiding the 'butter mountains' and 'wine lakes' of the 1980s when farmers produced simply to earn subsidy rather than for the market. Most of the support money is now given out based on the size of the farm, benefiting the biggest landowners, although there are increasing efforts to link payments to environmental targets. Other new rules require farms of a certain size to grow at least three different crops, while an 'active farmer' test will identify land being used as an airfield or golf course which received payments in the past. With an average age of sixty for hill farmers in Britain and a struggle generally to attract young people to work on the land, there will also be cash incentives to the under-forties who take on farms.

Despite the latest tweaks to the Common Agricultural Policy, the main British political parties remain fundamentally opposed to the unconditional way the EU hands out most of its farm funding. Both Labour and the Conservatives wanted to phase out direct payments by 2020 but were continually blocked by other countries. Britain has long argued for more open world trade, which would allow poorer countries easier access to sell their produce to Europe and stop subsidised European farmers distorting markets in other countries with artificially cheap goods that make it harder for local farmers to make a living. As explained in the Prosperity chapter, the average British household pays an annual premium of €324 to subsidise farmers. The consumer would therefore seem to have much to gain from leaving the EU and its CAP but the farmer would have much to lose.

A unilateral decision to pull out of the EU would not end the need to hand public money to farmers to keep some of them afloat, especially given the precarious and volatile nature of world food prices, and the subsidies received by competitors in other countries. In fact, one reason why the Norwegians and the Swiss voted not to join the EU was because of pressure from their farmers to keep even more generous subsidies. The average EU payment across all types of farm in the UK was £25,000 in 2012–13. Lowland grazing farming was the poorest paid and most supported, with £15,600 of the average annual income of £16,500 coming from the CAP.[51] Non-EU Norway is not in the CAP and provides its farmers with 63 per cent of their average income, the highest level of state support in the world, while Switzerland gives the second-highest global hand-out of 57 per cent of average farm earnings, according to the OECD. Farmers in the EU received an average of 19 per cent of their income from Brussels in 2012, close to the OECD average of 18.5 per cent, but higher than the 13.5 per cent in Russia, 7.1 per cent in the US and 2.7 per cent in Australia.

The UKIP response is attractive – simply create a British system of farm payments to provide domestic farmers with the same level of support as the EU, drop the bureaucratic requirements, limit the annual maximum payout and pocket the difference from the UK's net subsidy to continental competitors of at least £2.2 billion a year. Farmers are a little more cautious. 'UKIP might succeed in getting the UK out in a referendum but they are not going to form the government and the main parties are opposed to subsidies and committed to phasing them out as soon as they can,' said

Martin Haworth, director of policy of the NFU. 'The
only thing that is stopping them is our membership of
the European Union. So the risk is that we would end up
outside the EU, still competing in the same markets we
are competing in, but without a subsidy.' UKIP wants to
end the current requirements to link around one-third of
the farm subsidy to environmental measures – which is
attractive to farmers but not a goal shared by the main
political parties. UKIP would be open to innovative
farming methods such as GM crops for an independent
Britain, although the Scottish government is strongly
opposed to this and there is also a lot of resistance in
Wales. Divisions over the use of GM technology at EU
level could be replicated between the home nations at
UK level in the event of British withdrawal.

Peter Kendall, President of the National Farmers'
Union, in an article for Regent's University in 2013, said:

> British farmers are, by and large, more favourable to
> the European Union than the generality of the British
> public. Eurosceptics often ascribe this, rather cynically,
> to the fact that they are subsidised by the EU. An histori-
> cal reminder is required here. The reason that there
> is a Common Agricultural Policy is that, in order to
> create a common market in farm goods, it was neces-
> sary to harmonise the various national agricultural
> policies to avoid trade distortions, real or perceived.
> For the National Farmers' Union, it is not the quantity
> of support that is important, it is equality of treatment
> with our competitors. Indeed, the NFU has stated that

it would be prepared to see support for farmers phased out, provided this happened equally across the European Union. Concerns about the distortions of competition which would occur if levels of support were to be very different are real, and of course would be particularly acute if they occurred on either side of a land border – say Ulster and the Republic of Ireland, or an independent Scotland inside the EU and England outside.

With 77 per cent of British food and non-alcoholic drink exports going to Europe, the NFU believes that its farmers would be better off inside the EU's Single Market, where the British minister and officials take part in setting the standards, and where they receive the same subsidies as their nearest competitors. More than one third of all lamb produced in the UK is exported to the EU. It is successful partly because it enters the EU duty free but if Britain was to move outside the Single Market, there is a risk that Brussels could apply its normal tariff of almost 40 per cent on foreign lamb imports. That would allow French farmers with their higher production costs a way back into the market. The NFU is wary of those who say that, because the UK has a trade deficit with the EU (it imports from Europe more than it exports), it would be in the EU's interests not to impose tariffs or other costs on British goods and risk a tit-for-tat trade war. Kendall continued:

The argument is frequently made that because we are net importers from the EU, it would not be in the interest of other members of the EU to see barriers to trade erected between the UK and the EU. From an agricultural point of view, at least, this is dubious. If the UK wishes to lower its tariff barriers with the rest of the world it would not, under WTO rules, be able to apply higher barriers to the EU. So the ability of the EU to export to the UK would be protected; the reverse would not apply.

The concerns of farmers at their fate if Britain left the EU are understandable. They could benefit like all businesses from a reduction in red tape and form-filling, and avoid some aggravating measures such as the EU requirement for electronic tagging of sheep, brought in to track animals following the foot and mouth outbreak, which is expensive to implement. 'The process of legislating a very detailed common policy by twenty-eight governments in co-decision with the European Parliament is extremely cumbersome and often easily open to criticism and even ridicule,' said Kendall.

The proposition that outside the EU we could devise a policy which was simpler, cleaner, less bureaucratic and more relevant is one that is bound to appear attractive. But that could also lead to negative developments as far as the farming community is concerned, if UK government support for the sector failed to deliver comparable outcomes for British farmers.

Farmers fear the loss of a British voice at the table when setting production standards, and above all they fear losing the kind of financial support and protection enjoyed by their nearest competitors. Their loss would be consumers' gain, with cheaper food likely to follow a British exit from the Common Agricultural Policy and withdrawal from the EU's Common External Tariff. This would lead to a period of tumbling prices and tough competition for British farmers. Ironically, a vote for greater British sovereignty from Brussels would almost certainly mean more foreign produce – at cheaper prices – on supermarket shelves.

FISHING

IN Britain manages its territorial waters extending twelve miles from its coast but the EU decides fishing quotas and negotiates access to neighbouring zones. Pushed by Britain, the EU agreed radical reforms in 2013 to the failed Common Fisheries Policy to phase out the vast amount of discarded fish.

OUT Britain regains sovereignty over its Exclusive Economic Zone extending 200 miles from its coast and can implement fish preservation measures to revive over-fished stocks. It would have to negotiate access rights to waters controlled by the EU, Norway, Iceland and Faroes.

KEY STATS 62 per cent of Atlantic stocks and 82 per cent of Mediterranean stocks are over-fished compared to 25 per cent worldwide; a million tonnes of mainly dead fish are thrown back every year; €2.73 billion was spent by the EU to scrap vessels between 1994 and 2013 and yet over-capacity increased by 3 per cent a year.[52]

From the deck of the Scottish trawler *Seagull*, the true obscenity of the EU's disastrous Common Fisheries Policy (CFP) was clear to see. Basket after basket of prime cod were thrown back dead into the North Sea off the Shetlands – not because there was anything wrong with them, but because the fishermen had already exceeded their EU quota for catching one of Britain's favourite fish. The *Seagull* was only allowed to bring back monkfish, megrim and ling. So all other types of dead or dying fish that did not meet strict EU criteria but had been captured in the nets as 'by-catch', such as the edible but unglamorous coley, were also dumped back into the sea. This was a scene from the hidden devastation of the CFP as revealed in 2011 by the celebrity chef Hugh Fearnley-Whittingstall in his TV series *Fish Fight*. 'I can't put a sign on the nets saying, "No cod today, please." I hate discarding fish,' said Gary Much, the skipper of the 400-tonne trawler. 'If we could land all the fish we catch, we could go to sea for half as many days, use half the fuel and no fish would be wasted. It is madness.' The EU estimated that one million tonnes of edible fish was simply thrown back every year by European fishermen. That was enough to supply all of Britain's fish and chip shops for a decade. Often the fishermen had caught less favoured fish and needed to make room on their boat or save their ice for more valuable ones. 'The crazy irony is that the quota system is meant to conserve fish stocks, particularly cod. But it seems obvious to me you cannot conserve fish by throwing a million tonnes of them back in the sea, dead,' said Fearnley-Whittingstall. Clearly the situation, which existed for thirty years, was ripe for reform but it took a campaign by a celebrity chef and a petition signed by 870,000 people to bring about change. The British government led the push for reform. 'It is indefensible. Imagine if farmers threw away half their lambs, cattle and pigs. There would be rioting in the streets,' said Richard Benyon, the fisheries minister. 'The current CFP has failed. It has not given us healthy fish stocks and it has not delivered a sustainable living for our fishing industry. Only genuine fundamental reform of this broken policy can turn around these failures.' The huge waste of discards seemed to sum up everything that was wrong with the EU's handling of its fisheries, with once plentiful species such as cod, bluefin tuna and anchovy fished almost to extinction in some areas as politicians overruled scientific advice when setting catch levels year in, year out. Fishing seemed one policy area where Britain would make a much better job of managing its own sovereign territory if it left the EU.

Almost three years on from the launch of the *Fish Fight* campaign, the unthinkable happened. In December 2013, the European Parliament voted in favour of a ban on discards of fish at sea following months of hard negotiations between ministers from the EU's fishing nations. Discards will be ended for shallow swimming species such as mackerel, herring and sardines from 2015, followed by deep swimmers such as cod, hake and sole from 2016. Only species that are known to have a good survival rate after being caught can be thrown back, all others must be landed. Young fish too small for normal sale will go as animal feed for a nominal price that does not encourage their capture, while fishermen who exceed their annual quota will have to buy spare allowances from their countrymen or have quotas reduced the following year. Among measures to monitor the discard ban, CCTV is being installed on some boats. This was not all – the discard ban was accompanied by a wider reform to ensure that scientific advice governs new catching limits known as Maximum Sustainable Yields, while more power was devolved to national authorities to allocate quotas and manage fleets in a process called regionalisation. The impressive reform package seemed to show that terrible EU policies could be changed, even if this one took three decades. 'We've got what we asked for,' said Fearnley-Whittingstall on his blog.

> Where the (crazy) old CFP said that fishermen had to discard fish that they didn't have quota for, the new CFP says that this is wasteful and every effort must go towards ending discards. It's a huge result for people power and sustainable policy-making. Massive thanks go out to everyone who signed up and got active, and to the politicians, fishermen, campaigners and scientists who have supported this cause.

There are warnings that the discard ban will not by itself save Europe's fishing industry and there are still tough decisions to be made on reducing the fleet capacity. But the story of the Common Fisheries Policy might yet have a happy ending. It has long been one of the most obvious EU powers that could be returned to national level, however, and the surprisingly enlightened reforms of 2013 have not changed the minds of some of those who cannot forgive the many years of inept top-down management from Brussels. The policy was originally dreamed up by the founding six member states when it became clear that the fishing nations of Ireland, Denmark and the UK were planning to join in 1973. The entry of Spain and Portugal in 1986 added vast extra territory and fleets, leading to chronic over-capacity which the EU did little to control. Politicians from the member states were put in charge of the final say on annual catch levels in a ritual Christmas showdown in Brussels which saw scientific advice routinely ignored. As a result of over-fishing, the annual catch of British fishermen is just one-tenth of what it was a century ago. In 2008, when 93 per cent of cod were caught before reaching the maturity required to breed, the EU set an even higher catch quota for the following year. Campaign groups still want a big cut in the EU fleet but the EU has already spent €2.73 billion on a scheme to 'buy out' fishermen and scrap their licences which actually saw fishing capacity rise because of the greater efficiency of the latest vessels, equipment and technology.

Britain's Exclusive Economic Zone, which covers all the sea and everything in it up to a distance of 200 nautical miles from its coast, is the largest of any EU country with the greatest range of fish species. The UK also has the second largest fisheries tonnage of the EU and the second largest processing industry. Regaining sovereignty over the sea, which is only possible by leaving the EU, would mean that Britain can close areas when stocks need time to regenerate and it can legally ban vessels from other nations. However, a block on one country's fishermen could lead to reciprocal measures on British fishermen in return and many of the most important fish, such as cod, herring, mackerel, plaice and whiting, migrate between several territorial areas during the course of their lives. As one fisherman's representative put it, crab and scallops are fairly sedentary but everything with a tail requires joint management with other jurisdictions. This has already triggered a new fishing war between the EU, Iceland and the Faroes, with the northern nations claiming the right to catch much more mackerel in recent years as the fish migrate into their areas in larger numbers, possibly due to sea warming, and threaten other stocks. 'The UK would clearly have a critical interest in ensuring that appropriate conservation policies were applied to those "straddling" stocks in order to avoid their being damaged by overfishing by other countries' vessels,' said Andy Lebrecht, the former UK deputy permanent representative in Brussels in an essay for Regent's University in 2013.

The only way to achieve this would be to enter into formal fisheries agreements with the EU and with Norway to deliver 'joint management', along the lines of the current EU–Norway agreement for the North Sea. Indeed, article 63 of the UN Conference of the Law of the Sea requires coastal states to do precisely this. Any negotiated joint management agreements would of necessity have to specify the share out of the stocks concerned. It is moreover all but certain that the other member states (and Norway) would insist on their current 'relative stability' shares of the Total Allowable Catches concerned and access to the UK's Exclusive Economic Zone (as now) as part of any such agreement. Given that the 'relative stability' settlement has endured for thirty years and was itself based on historic fishing patterns, it is difficult to see how the UK could articulate a convincing argument for any alternative allocation of fishing rights.

Shared fishing stocks are a biological reality of the seas and a failure to agree joint management plans with neighbouring authorities such as Norway, Iceland and the EU could result in a free-for-all, which would inevitably lead to overfishing. Exports to Europe could also become subject to the EU's Common External Tariff depending on the trade deal that Britain ends up negotiating with Brussels after leaving.

Until the recent EU reforms, the case for Britain claiming back its historic fishing grounds was overwhelming. After many years of failure, the Common Fisheries Policy may have been saved, in no small part thanks to the efforts of British fishermen and ministers, from a system that had become politicised and detached from science, best practice and local needs. Barry Deas, of the National Federation of Fishermen's Organisations, said:

> Only time will tell if regionalisation will become an effective counterweight to central control in Brussels, which has been really the reason why the Common Fisheries Policy has been so ineffectual on the conservation front. The model of command and control is thoroughly discredited and a move towards decentralisation is recognised as necessary to lay the foundations of a more effective policy.

As for the move to end discards, he added:

> What it will mean in practice, everybody including the
> scientists and the industry are scratching their heads
> over implementing it successfully on the ground. This
> is certainly going to be destabilising because in many
> ways it turns things on its head – for example, one of
> the fisheries with a high level of discards is plaice, but
> plaice stocks are doing very well despite the high level
> of discards and one of the reasons is that quite a high
> proportion of them survive, maybe 60 per cent, when
> you put them back. If you now are obliged to take them
> ashore, dead, they are not going to be contributing to the
> biomass. Everybody wants to reduce discards but it is
> just not as straightforward as some people think.

Norway kept control over its fisheries after deciding
not to join the EU in 1973 and has had its own discard
ban since 1987. It has negotiated access for its fishermen to EU waters and vice versa, with the EU making
Norway's access to the Single Market conditional upon
allowing European vessels to fish in Norwegian waters.
It is far too soon to tell if the EU's reorganised Common
Fisheries Policy will provide the modernised and responsible fishing industry that consumers want. But it makes
the decision to leave the EU based on fishing concerns a
little less clear-cut than it has been for decades.

JUSTICE

IN Britain has the right to opt out of all 133 EU justice policies agreed before the Lisbon Treaty of 2009 and can opt back into those it wants to join such as the European Arrest Warrant (EAW) and the police cooperation agency Europol.

OUT Fast-track extradition would no longer be possible to or from the EU countries without the EAW and cases could be held up for years. Britain could apply to join Europol just like non-EU members Norway and Switzerland which cooperate fully and have liaison officers at the headquarters.

KEY STATS From 2009 to 2013, 507 suspects were sent to the UK using the EAW including sixty-three for child sex offences, 105 for drug trafficking and forty-four for murder; 4,005 suspects were extradited from the UK using EAWs to other EU states, including fifty-seven for child sex offences, 414 for drug trafficking and 105 for murder.

Rachid Ramda, an Algerian granted asylum in Britain, was the UK's longest-serving extradition prisoner by the time he was finally deported in 2005 to face terrorism charges laid ten years earlier in France, following a series of bomb attacks on the Paris Metro that left eight dead and 170 injured. The case caused diplomatic tensions between Britain and France as Ramda's lawyers, funded by Legal Aid, launched a series of appeals to delay his deportation. He was eventually jailed in France for ten years for association with a terrorist organisation. Cases like this helped to convince EU justice and home affairs ministers to agree a fast-track extradition measure, the European Arrest Warrant (EAW), following the 9/11 attacks in the US. It was hailed as a breakthrough in the fight against terror. 'There will be nowhere in Europe for terrorists to hide,' wrote Peter Hain, the Europe Minister, in October 2001. In stark contrast to the Ramda case, Hussain Osman, one of the would-be London bombers in the failed attacks of 21 July 2005, was seized on a European Arrest Warrant by Italian police in Rome and extradited back to Britain less than two months after he fled the country. It was not just terrorists, however, who were targeted by the warrant. By far the highest number of EAWs are issued by former Communist countries with very different justice systems to Britain: Poland tops the list with 1,659 warrants (until the end of March 2011) followed by Lithuania (355), and the Czech Republic (162). Suspects have been demanded under these fast-track measures for the theft of two car tyres, possession of 0.45g of cannabis and piglet-rustling (in Lithuania). Under the terms of the warrant, the country receiving the demand cannot normally refuse to make an arrest and hand over the suspect. Besides the trivial cases, the group Fair Trials International has campaigned to raise awareness of a growing number of miscarriages of justice involving Britons. Edmond Arapi was targeted by an Italian EAW to serve sixteen years in prison after being convicted *in absentia* of a murder in Genoa, a city he had never visited and which took place on a day he was at work in a café in Leek in Staffordshire. Italy only dropped the EAW after he had spent weeks in custody and several months on strict bail conditions. Andrew Symeou was extradited to Greece in July 2009 in connection with the death of a man at a nightclub, despite evidence that the charges were based on statements extracted by Greek police through intimidation of witnesses who later retracted their statements. Symeou was bailed after spending more than ten months in a Greek prison and was not finally cleared until June 2011. Deborah Dark was acquitted of drug offences in France in 1989 but, unknown to her, French prosecutors appealed and a two-year jail sentence was imposed in her absence. She was arrested in 2006 and only after a three-year legal ordeal was the case dropped. Patrick Connor (a pseudonym) was arrested in Spain with two friends in connection with two counterfeit €50 notes found in the apartment where they were staying. Released and returned to the UK, he was arrested under an EAW four years later and extradited back to Spain. He was held in a maximum security prison in Madrid and faced the prospect of a two-year wait in pre-trial detention. Although he maintained he had no knowledge of the counterfeit notes, he decided to plead guilty to reduce his time being held and spent nine weeks in prison before coming home to finish his studies with his life blighted by a criminal record. The potential dangers of the EAW, as well as its fundamental clash with the principles of British justice, were highlighted by a former member of the Commons Home Affairs Select

Committee during the passage of the 2003 Extradition Bill which enshrined the warrant into British law. The young MP spoke out against the way that it abolished the principle of 'dual criminality' by obliging EU states to extradite suspects for misdemeanours that are not considered criminal offences in the arresting country's own law. 'We are in new territory here. Never before have we given up the dual criminality protection,' David Cameron told the Commons while still a backbencher. 'I believe that we are making a great mistake … It is an important safeguard that people in this country have had for years.'

EU involvement in criminal justice measures has long been a bone of contention between Britain and Brussels despite a general acceptance that the police in Europe need to work closely together to combat complicated cases of cross-border crime. A clear policy of inter-governmental cooperation was set down in the Maastricht Treaty to ensure that member states retained a veto over measures that encroached on their own traditions of criminal justice. However, just fifteen years later the Lisbon Treaty dramatically increased EU control over policing and criminal law, moving the entire policy area into the realm of Qualified Majority Voting and oversight by the European Court of Justice. Because this was such a significant shift from a situation so carefully negotiated by British diplomats at Maastricht to avoid making British justice subject to a higher EU legal authority, the UK was given a one-off opportunity to decide whether to retain or reject all of the policing and criminal justice measures passed before the Lisbon Treaty entered into force. The government had until June 2014 to decide whether to opt out of 133 separate items, including the European Arrest Warrant, and afterwards negotiate to re-enter individual provisions on a case-by-case basis, at the risk of extra conditions being imposed by the EU. It was a golden opportunity in the eyes of Conservative backbenchers to repatriate powers from Brussels.

Theresa May, the Home Secretary, outlined a plan to exercise the block opt-out and opt back into thirty-five policies deemed to be in the national interest, despite their move to tighter EU control. These include the EAW as well as membership of Eurojust and Europol, two organisations based in The Hague. Eurojust, set up in 2002, exists to foster cooperation between national prosecuting authorities in crimes that concern more than one EU state. Member nations are obliged to provide Eurojust with 'any information necessary for the performance of its tasks'. The Lisbon Treaty has introduced the possibility of enabling Eurojust to initiate criminal investigations. Europol, the European Police Office headed by Rob Wainwright, a Welshman, became operational in 1999 and collects, stores, analyses and exchanges information, while also having the power to ask member states to initiate, conduct or coordinate criminal investigations. Europol and Eurojust coordination has been central to breaking international drugs and people-trafficking gangs as well as two global paedophile rings in joint police investigations known as Operation Koala and Operation Rescue. Koala began when a child abuse video was discovered in Australia that had been made in Belgium by an Italian producer with 2,500 global customers. It led to coordinated arrests including men in trusted positions, such as teachers and swimming instructors, as well as the identification of twenty-three children aged under sixteen. Operation Rescue led to the arrest of 184 suspected paedophiles, including 121 in the UK, when Dutch police seized the servers of a chatroom after British police traced two perpetrators to Spain and discovered their use of the website. The three-year operation across thirty countries led to the rescue of 230 children, including sixty in the UK. These are the kind of transnational inquiries which show the benefits of EU coordination.

The Fresh Start group of Conservative MPs has called for Britain to take the opportunity of the Lisbon Treaty opt-out to withdraw completely from the field of criminal justice involvement with the EU. 'The UK has a unique legal tradition and should not be subject to ECJ rulings in the area of Policing and Criminal Justice (PCJ),' the group said in its manifesto in November 2013. 'The Lisbon Treaty provided the UK with an option to opt out of 133 EU laws, which the government plans to invoke. We should go further and opt out of all EU PCJ laws entirely, and pursue operational cooperation with the EU via other means.' Bilateral cooperation would be possible with Europol, which works closely with non-EU members Norway and Switzerland, and has officials from these two countries permanently based at Europol headquarters. But other measures, such as the European Arrest Warrant, would be difficult to recreate on a voluntary basis. The Fresh Start proposal was dismissed by the Liberal Democrat spokeswoman on justice, Sarah Ludford.

> These proposals would indeed be a fresh start, for the thousands of criminals who would find it far easier to escape justice. Pulling out of EU crime-fighting measures altogether would be a gift to drug-smugglers, human-traffickers and online sex offenders. The European Arrest Warrant does need reform, but we should not throw the baby out with the bath water. It remains a vital crime-fighting tool that has prevented thousands of criminals from escaping the long arm of the law.

The Association of Chief Police Officers (ACPO) called the EAW the most important of all the EU measures. In parliamentary evidence, it wrote:

> Recent data gathered by the Metropolitan Police Service (MPS) in the first quarter of 2012 showed that of 61,939 people arrested in London, 8,089 were nationals from EU countries (13 per cent) and 9,358 were foreign nationals from outside the EU (15 per cent). In 2011–12 the MPS received fifty EAWs for homicide, twenty for rape, and ninety for robbery. Each of these cases represents a person who is wanted for a serious crime who fled to the UK. There is strong evidence to show that foreign criminals who come to the UK continue to offend when in the UK. There is a real risk that opting out of the EAW and relying on less effective extradition

arrangements could have the effect of turning the UK into a 'safe haven' for Europe's criminals.

By including the European Arrest Warrant in the measures Britain wanted to retain, Theresa May also agreed to accept another controversial EU justice measure, the European Supervision Order (ESO), as a safeguard against mistreatment. The ESO is an alternative to pre-trial detention and allows the home state of the suspect to request supervision measures rather than see its citizens locked up for months, like Andrew Symeou. The British government had long been in two minds about agreeing it because the UK receives far more EAW requests than it makes. It was a demonstration of how a further EU measure was thought necessary to ameliorate an earlier one.

But the British government refused point blank to sign up to another criminal justice measure provided for in the Lisbon Treaty and proposed by the European Commission in 2013 – a European Public Prosecutor. This office, run through Eurojust, would 'be responsible for investigating, prosecuting and bringing to judgment … the perpetrators of, and accomplices in, offences against the Union's financial interests', according to the treaty. Although Britain has made clear it will opt out, the European Public Prosecutor can go ahead under 'enhanced agreement' by at least nine member states. The Lisbon Treaty also made provision for the EPP's role to be expanded in the future 'to include serious cross-border crime', suggesting the foundations of a common

EU system of criminal justice. 'There is nothing wrong with practical cooperation with other European countries on policing and criminal justice matters, especially when crime is increasingly international,' said Theresa May in July 2013. 'But there is no reason at all for a European Public Prosecutor or anything like a European police force. We will make sure that Britain does not participate and will not come under the jurisdiction of any such prosecutor.' Britain has consistently been a reluctant partner in EU justice and policing measures. It will try to avoid the most intrusive developments if it stays in the EU, and will try to cooperate on the most vital measures if it leaves.

OVERSEAS AID

IN The UK counts the proportion of its EU membership fee spent on overseas development towards its national aid target of 0.7 per cent of gross national income (GNI). In 2012, £1.1 billion of the £8.77 billion spent on aid by the UK was managed through the European Commission, comprising £780 million through the EU budget and £327 million through the European Development Fund.[53]

OUT Britain could keep its target of spending 0.7 per cent of GNI on overseas development and could still coordinate spending with the European Commission, or it could divert the £1.1 billion that goes to aid through Brussels back to domestic spending.

KEY STATS Britain is the world's second most generous international donor country by amount and sixth most generous by percentage of GNI. The EU and its member states together provided €55.2 billion in international aid in 2012, more than half of the global total and 0.43 per cent of collective gross national income. The EU itself handed out €9.54 billion from its budget. The top recipient was Turkey with €419 million, then the Palestinian Territories with €247 million, Afghanistan €200 million, Ethiopia €193 million and Serbia €186 million.[54]

The South African government reacted angrily when Britain announced in 2013 that it would end direct aid to the country in 2015. Although the annual grant was only £19 million, a tiny fraction of the UK's £8.77 billion annual overseas development spending, Pretoria's Department of International Relations said that it was 'tantamount to redefining our relationship'. Partly this was because it brought an abrupt end to an era of British assistance for a close fellow Commonwealth member, and partly it was because South Africa felt itself a victim of domestic political wrangling over the aid budget after surviving a cull of British partners in 2011, which ended assistance to Angola, Bosnia and Herzegovina, Burundi, Cameroon, Cambodia, China, Gambia, Indonesia, Iraq, Kosovo, Lesotho, Moldova, Niger, Russia, Serbia and Vietnam. They were followed by India in another sudden announcement in 2012 that the £280 million annual transfer from the UK would end in 2015. These countries were now deemed to fall into the 'middle income' category or even 'upper middle income' and in times of hardship the UK government decided to focus its overseas aid strategically on reducing poverty in twenty-six of the world's poorest and most fragile countries. The writing had been on the wall for months for India after its finance minister Pranab Mukherjee, later the country's President, said that Britain's aid payment was 'a peanut in our total development expenditure'. In contrast to South Africa, the Indian External Affairs Minister Salman Khurshid accepted the British decision by declaring that 'aid is past, trade is future'. Britain's aid budget will be kept at the ring-fenced level of 0.7 per cent of gross national income, one of only five EU countries (all rich northerners) to reach the level set as a target for 2015. 'South Africa has made enormous progress over the past two decades, to the extent that it is now the region's economic powerhouse and Britain's biggest trading partner in Africa. South Africa is now in a position to fund its own development,' said Justine Greening, the International Development Secretary. 'It is right that our relationship changes to one of mutual co-operation and trade.' Aid agencies disagreed. Melanie Ward of ActionAid said:

> The UK, and particularly David Cameron, rightly state a desire to end extreme poverty. This is incredibly important, but running away from middle-income countries where 80 per cent live on less than $2 a day is the wrong way to make this happen. This is the wrong decision, at the wrong time. It is particularly concerning since it comes hot on the heels of the UK announcing its early withdrawal of aid from India.

Some British funding will still find its way to most of the countries on the list of those being dropped by the Department for International Development (DFID), however. That is because they will get cash from the European Union. The proportion of Britain's EU membership fee related to EU aid spending is counted towards the national development spending target, as is the money sent from DFID to the European Development Fund (EDF), an intergovernmental agreement by the EU states outside the EU budget, beyond the control of the European Parliament and the main vehicle for EU funding of African, Caribbean and Pacific countries. In 2012–13, £1.1 billion spent on aid by the UK was managed through the European Commission, made up of £780 million through the EU budget and

£327 million through the EDF. But even in Brussels, the winds of change are blowing through its huge overseas aid budget in a major shake-up that could also see both South Africa and India losing out on annual direct funding.

Britain's commitment to spending 0.7 per cent of national wealth on international aid has been controversial among politicians, mainly on the Right, who believe that the money would be better off spent on schools and healthcare in the UK. Lord Ashcroft, the Tory peer, said that many Conservatives found the level of aid spending 'morally wrong' when the government was cutting domestic budgets. He sent an open letter to Ms Greening on her appointment to urge her to 'turn off the golden taps and stop flooding the developing world with our money'. Conservatives argued that India's decision to choose French Mirage jets over UK-made Typhoons showed that aid spending was not bringing Britain associated political benefits. Godfrey Bloom, the former UK Independence Party MEP, had his own criticism of overseas aid. 'How we can possibly be giving a billion pounds a month, when we're in this sort of debt, to Bongo Bongo Land is completely beyond me,' he was filmed telling party activists. 'To buy Ray-Ban sunglasses, apartments in Paris, Ferraris and all the rest of it that goes with most of the foreign aid. F18s for Pakistan. We need a new squadron of F18s. Who's got the squadrons? Pakistan, where we send the money.' Bloom was asked by his party to stop using the phrase Bongo Bongo Land but insisted that he was not being racist. 'If anybody would care to take a look at the Oxford dictionary ... they would find bongo is a white antelope that lives in the forest,' he said. Bloom told *The Times* he had received three letters of support from Africa for his remarks and asked, 'Is my mailbag lying to me?'

Yet even Kofi Annan, the former United Nations Secretary General, supported calls for Britain and the EU to stop giving billions of pounds in aid to wealthier countries.

> The emerging markets and the countries that are doing well should wean themselves off aid. Countries like Brazil, China, India, Ghana, Guatemala and Honduras – some of these countries can fend for themselves. In fact, I have had the chance to suggest to some of them that they should not accept Britain's aid willingly. They need to say 'We are full enough', so that there will be more money available for the really poor and weaker.

The EU's treaties give it the power to conduct a common policy in overseas aid and humanitarian assistance without preventing its member states from conducting their own actions in these areas. The top priority of the EU is to 'foster the sustainable economic, social and environmental development of developing countries, with the primary aim of eradicating poverty'. This is a good fit with Britain's overarching aims in the areas of development cooperation and humanitarian aid which are,

respectively, to eliminate poverty and to respond effectively to disasters. The treaties also require the EU to

> contribute to peace, security, the sustainable develop-
> ment of the earth, solidarity and mutual respect among
> peoples, free and fair trade, eradication of poverty and
> the protection of human rights, in particular the rights
> of the child as well as to the strict observance and the
> development of international law, including respect for
> the principles of the United Nations Charter.

The European Consensus on Development agreed in
2006 stated that the overarching aim of EU development
policy was to reduce poverty worldwide by achieving the
Millennium Development Goals (MDGs), a set of eight
targets agreed at the United Nations in 2000 for 2015.
However, some of the world's poorest countries are a
long way off the key MDGs, causing Britain's review
of aid partners to focus funds and triggering a rethink
in Brussels. The first sign of this was the European
Commission's Agenda for Change review of 2011 which
also began to suggest that 'Middle Income Countries'
like India and South Africa should lose direct aid as
their economies continued to grow. Resources should
be targeted 'where they are needed most to address
poverty reduction and where they could have the greatest impact' and 'grant-based aid should not feature in
geographic cooperation with more advanced developing
countries'. In turning round the supertanker of EU aid
policy, at a time of a global rethink with the approach of

the 2015 deadline for MDGs, it signalled a shift to assistance based on good governance, democracy and human rights, linked to greater conditionality; and also based on growth, with a strong focus on leveraging private sector money. Neighbouring countries, especially those ambitious to join the EU, will continue to receive generous support from Brussels, which is why Britain could end its direct payments to Bosnia, Moldova, Serbia and Kosovo in the knowledge that the UK will actually still be funding development through its contribution to the EU budget.

It is easy for the media to find bizarre projects and mis-spent funds in the EU's vast overseas funding operation, with €58.7 billion earmarked for the 2014–20 budget period, a rise of 3.3 per cent on the previous seven years. In 2012, the *Sunday Telegraph* highlighted the fact that the EU spent around half of its aid budget on middle-income countries, with £30 million spent that year in China on twenty-two projects, £10 million in Brazil, £9.5 million in Argentina and £40 million in Russia, including £240,000 for an arts project in St Petersburg. Iceland received £4.2 million including £400,000 for a scheme to promote tourism in Katla national park while projects in Turkey, the biggest recipient of EU aid, included funding for a TV series about the EU. The paper did not mention the EU's Food Facility programme which paid for the inoculation of 44.6 million livestock in the poorest countries, the €25 million spent towards a solar power plant in Burkina Faso to provide power to 400,000 people, or the programme to provide basic primary education to 40,000 Somali children and train 4,000 primary and secondary school teachers in Somalia.[55] The European Commission's overseas aid directorate said:

> Investing in external assistance is a smart investment, with a long-term vision. The EU and its partners have a mutual interest in making sure poverty steps back: less poverty means less trafficking, less illegal migration, less pandemics, less terrorism and insecurity. It is cheaper to eliminate root causes of the problem than to deal with the symptoms further down the line. In the current context, it makes more sense than ever to improve coordination of all member states' aid: we will avoid duplication and get the highest impact.

But while DFID rated aid delivered through the European Development Fund as 'very good value for money' because of its 'strong poverty focus with 85 per cent of funds going to lower income countries', delivery through the EU budget was only rated 'adequate value for money for UK aid' because 'a significant share of resources goes to middle income countries and focus on MDGs is mixed; procedures are inflexible'.

Development cooperation was the subject of one of the first batch of the government's assessment of Britain's relationship with the EU known as the Review of the Balance of Consequences and published in July 2013. The consensus of most respondents was that 'while there is a need for improvement in many areas of EU activity, the advantages of working through the EU outweigh the disadvantages', according to the government's summary. The Trades Union Congress (TUC), for example, said that the UK gained enormously from involvement in EU development cooperation and humanitarian assistance. In its view, criticism levelled at the EU 'makes the case for improvement, not repatriation' of powers to the national level. If these powers were repatriated to the UK, 'the UK would achieve less with its expenditure than it did now, and the activities of EU member states put together would also achieve less'. Only two out of fifty-one submissions questioned the value of working through the EU in development cooperation. Open Europe called for a more flexible approach, recommending that national contributions to the EU aid budget should be made entirely voluntary on a similar basis to the European Development Fund (EDF). The Freedom Association argued that EU aid spending has been wasteful, ineffective and harmful to the UK's objectives. It argued that the UK could achieve its development goals more effectively if it were to take more action bilaterally, or even through other multilateral channels independent of the EU. Outside the EU, the Swiss Agency for Development and Cooperation (SDC), told the review that it had an input into EU aid policy debates through contacts with the European Commission as well as a close working relationship with four key donor countries in the EU including the UK. 'There is a high degree of coincidence between SDC's new development strategy 2013–16 and DFID's business plan 2012–15,' wrote Martin Dahinden, SDC director-general. Shared priorities included 'strong engagement in the post-2015 development agenda, efforts to combat climate change and water scarcity, a commitment to better governance of natural resources, and an impartial and independent humanitarian aid'. Switzerland established its development priorities in consultation with the European Commission, he added, to make sure its aid effort was aligned with the EU. This would almost certainly be the case if Britain were to leave the EU, especially given that both Labour in government and the Conservative-led coalition have been keen to commit to generous aid spending both through Brussels and bilaterally.

TRANSPORT

IN British airlines are able to fly not only to and from other EU states but also between airports within those states. Budget airlines owe their existence to EU deregulation.

OUT British airlines would have to renegotiate both intra-EU flight rights and transatlantic slots. Its road hauliers would still have to comply with EU rules on safety, size, loading and drivers' hours when working on the continent.

KEY STATS Heathrow is the EU's busiest airport with 70 million passengers in 2012, followed by Paris Charles De Gaulle (61.6 million) and Frankfurt (57.5 million).[56] Dover is the EU's busiest passenger port and Felixstowe the seventh busiest container port. Almost 20 million passengers and 20.2 million tonnes of freight travelled through the Channel Tunnel in 2012.[57] 56 per cent of easyJet's 60.8 million passengers in 2012-13 were from outside the UK.[58]

The Irish government refused to allow Tony Ryan's new airline permission to fly from Dublin to Luton in order to protect the national carrier, Aer Lingus, from competition on the lucrative route between Ireland and Britain. Margaret Thatcher's government had other ideas. The British Prime Minister had pushed for the Single Market which ushered in the 'double disapproval' regime, meaning that authorities in both countries had to object to stop an airline opening up flights between them. It was a weakening of national sovereignty that Thatcher very much approved of. Ryanair was given the green light to fly to Luton by the British authorities and ended up eventually becoming bigger than Aer Lingus and embroiled in a long-running battle to take it over. Ironically, the EU authorities blocked this on the grounds of maintaining healthy competition in the interests of consumers. Successive rounds of EU deregulation broke down national airline monopolies and made it possible for Ryanair and its British rival easyJet to get off the ground. They are now Europe's two biggest low-cost carriers. 'EasyJet is a child of the EU,' said the company's spokesman. 'Essentially aviation was controlled by each sovereign state and easyJet broke down historic sovereignty-based agreements.' Michael O'Leary, the outspoken chief executive of Ryanair, put it like this: 'We've liberated people to fly. We've done more for European integration than any other company. We've probably prevented wars breaking out because we make it easier for young kids to spend time travelling abroad.' The benefits for consumers have been substantial. Before Ryanair came along in 1986, it cost £170 to fly from Dublin to London return with either Aer Lingus or British Airways, the only two options. Ryanair immediately halved the price, forcing its rivals to cut fares too. The era of budget air travel had dawned and has been one of the great success stories of the EU's Single Market. The European Common Aviation Area means that an airline based in any member state can fly between any two airports in the EU, including between airports within a single EU country. Most countries jealously guard their airspace rights, which is why

European airlines cannot fly between US cities and US airlines cannot fly from one European airport to another European airport. Despite Michael O'Leary once calling the European Commission the 'evil empire' when it challenged subsidies apparently provided by Charleroi airport in Belgium, Ryanair showed its support for the EU by putting €500,000 of the company's money towards the campaign for a 'yes' vote for the Lisbon Treaty in Ireland's 2009 rerun referendum.

Cheap airline travel is one clear benefit of the EU that is probably here to stay thanks to the level of intense competition unleashed by the Single Market and pioneered most aggressively by Ryanair. The biggest immediate impact of Brexit is likely to be on British airlines and their ability to hold on to lucrative overseas routes, including across the Atlantic, and this in turn could affect fares depending on the final outcome of lengthy and difficult renegotiations. In order to keep the status quo, the UK would either have to follow non-member Norway into the European Economic Area (EEA) which will maintain access to the European Common Aviation Area (ECAA) or negotiate from outside the EEA to stay in the ECAA, membership of which has to be ratified by every EU member state. In either case, Britain would then have to agree to the full application of EU aviation law and abide by decisions taken by the EU affecting how the ECAA is run without having a vote on them. ECAA membership gives British airlines cabotage rights – the ability to fly between EU airports without having to start or end at a British airport. Without membership of the ECAA, easyJet would still be able to fly from the UK to a European destination and back again but the loss of intra-EU routes would probably force it to create a new subsidiary based inside the EU if it wanted to carry on with those flights. Such a split into two companies could have an impact on fares and on employment levels at easyJet's Luton base. Ryanair, which is headquartered in Ireland, would still be able to fly to and from the UK.

Leaving the EU would also require British airlines to renegotiate transatlantic routes which have been agreed in an EU-wide package between Brussels and the US. Brexit would signal a period of turbulence for airlines and government aviation officials with the EU and beyond. 'If the UK was willing to accept every aspect of the [EU] single aviation market, it would presumably be possible to negotiate reciprocal access,' wrote Handley Stevens, former Under Secretary at the Ministry of Transport in an essay for Regent's University.

However, air service negotiations are famous for hard bargaining, and European airlines which had lost market share to UK airlines (notably to easyJet) might well look for ways to restore their competitive edge, for example by insisting that UK airlines could only fly to and from the UK. The renegotiation of bilateral rights with third countries such as the USA could be even more difficult. The rights of UK airlines under EU agreements would expire if not with immediate effect from the date of withdrawal, when BA and Virgin Atlantic would cease to be

EU airlines, then at best after the usual period of twelve months' notice. Moreover, in any renegotiations arising from such a disengagement, against a tight deadline which might apply to a large number of simultaneous negotiations, it cannot be assumed that the third countries concerned would necessarily be prepared to grant unchanged rights to UK airlines under a new bilateral treaty without demanding significant additional benefits for their own airlines in exchange.

The ultimate impact on the consumer is unclear, and may be minimal, but the upheaval for the airlines could be considerable.

For travel by road, British companies that run commercial vehicles on the continent would still have to comply with EU rules for driver working hours and rest periods, as well as the common regulations for pollution and vehicle weight and size, notwithstanding any changes to these rules for Britain's roads after leaving the EU. The British government has already rejected so-called 'super lorries' measuring up to 25.25 metres long after the European Commission left it up to national authorities to decide whether to allow lorries beyond the existing 18.75 metres and 44 tonnes gross vehicle weight maximums. One advantage of leaving the EU claimed by anti-EU campaigners would be to charge foreign lorries to drive on British roads. Charging road users is not illegal under EU law at the moment, provided that the charge is also paid by domestic drivers. Following pressure from the Bavarian Christian Social

Union party in the ruling German coalition, the government elected in September 2013 is planning to charge foreign vehicles and find a way to compensate domestic road users, probably by a lower road tax. It remains to be seen whether the European Commission will challenge this blatant attempt to circumvent the spirit of EU law. If an independent Britain brought in a surcharge on European lorries while exempting its own, the European Commission has made it clear that there would probably be repercussions. 'If the UK, in the event that it was outside the EU, decided to introduce legislation which discriminates against foreigners, it would expose itself to the risk of countervailing measures from the EU member states, which could end up being very costly for British hauliers,' said an official at the European Commission transport directorate.

Transport policy is one area where a supra-national body like the EU has a genuine role in facilitating common standards for a continent criss-crossed by rail services, roads, waterways and aviation routes. While the impact of Brexit would be felt most keenly in the aviation sector, which has the highest international dimension of British transport, it would have much less effect on other modes of transport where the vast majority of journeys begin and end in the UK. For travel by train, the UK only has two international routes (through the Channel Tunnel and from Belfast to Dublin) covered primarily by several international agreements including the Intergovernmental Organisation for International Carriage by Rail (OTIF), originally founded in 1893 and of which Britain is one of forty-eight members. This sets basic rules for technical standards, compensation for delayed passengers and carriage of dangerous goods. For travel by sea, general standards for safety, training, pollution and working conditions are set globally by the International Maritime Organisation (which the UK has been a member of since 1949) and the International Labour Organisation (of which the UK was a founder member in 1919). In contrast to the potentially massive upheaval for UK-based airlines, British sea and rail travel would not change much in the event of Brexit.

CONCLUSION

A referendum on the European Union took place early in 2014 that gave a foretaste of the public vote likely to happen in Britain within the next few years. By the narrowest of margins – 50.3 per cent to 49.7 per cent – the Swiss decided to reimpose quotas on migrants from the EU. This was, of course, Switzerland's democratic right as a nation that had long ago decided to stay outside the EU in order to retain significant control over its domestic affairs. But the closeness of the outcome and its potential implications showed the dilemma facing voters in an independent-minded European country when asked to choose between two powerful and competing forces.

On one side was the economic argument, backed by most of the political parties and big businesses, that the unrestricted movement of people across the border not only maintained good relations with the neighbours but was a key reason for Switzerland's high standards of living. On the other side was the defence of national identity and self governance, less tangible but equally potent concerns, championed by populist politicians warning that the country was being overwhelmed by high numbers of incomers and undermined by outside interference from Brussels. The Swiss knew full well that voting against the freedom of movement of people – a principle held sacred by the EU – would damage a range of other agreements. Nevertheless, the protection of sovereignty narrowly triumphed over the economic advantages of open borders. This was a microcosm of the choice which will face British voters in a referendum on EU membership.

Belonging to the EU has always been a trade-off between the surrender of national controls and the economic, political, social and cultural benefits of 'ever closer union' with the continent. In 1973 when Britain joined, and in 1975 when the British voted in a referendum to stay in what was then known as the European Economic Community, there was a different balance to the equation. The UK was one of nine western European member states with more or less similar standards of living, economic prospects and expectations. The legal and judicial processes of the nine varied in style and rigour but within tolerable limits, and it made sense to defer to a higher authority (the European Commission) to propose common laws to apply to all the members and also to adjudicate (the European Court of Justice) on disputes concerning the shared powers. Each country had a veto over any European proposals which it felt would damage its core national interests. The world was a much more hostile and protectionist place for trade so it made perfect sense to join a club of like-minded partners to open up congruous markets and build shared defences in a customs union. On this scale, Europe's four freedoms – of goods, capital, services and people – were logical and bold principles to expand each national economy in step with the others. The nine member states would develop in harmony and through the harmonisation of trading rules and regulations. This world would not last for long.

What happened over the next couple of decades was truly historic and a cause for celebration across a continent blighted for centuries by warring foes and autocratic regimes. Spain, Portugal and Greece threw off dictatorships to join the European club of nations, followed by eleven former Communist countries escaping decades of repression. Every nation in the entire continent west of Russia applied to join the European Union with the exception of Belarus, Moldova, Ukraine and several microstates. Only in Norway and Switzerland was membership narrowly rejected in referendums – while there is still an orderly queue of eastern applicants including Montenegro, Macedonia, Serbia, Albania and Turkey. The expansion, combined with a dogmatic adherence to the principle of the four freedoms, brought tensions within the wealthier western members, which were exacerbated from 2008 onwards by the long economic downturn. Opposition grew to the influx of people from the newest member states who had lower expectations of pay and living conditions. Nowhere was this antagonism more politically charged than in Britain, where the UK Independence Party harnessed a mood of dissatisfaction with the pace of change in the EU, and a large section of the ruling Conservative Party demanded a reordering of Britain's relationship to scale back the powers handed to Brussels. The UK was not alone in voicing concern – the centre-right Dutch government called for an end to the credo of 'ever closer union' written into the founding Treaty of Rome in 1957. Conservative politicians in Germany also raised questions about the level of EU regulation and the unfettered right of migration, while eurosceptic movements gathered in strength in many other member countries.

David Cameron presented his promise of a refer-endum on the EU in 2017 as a general call for reform of the organisation. This could not disguise the fact that the UK was the main country demanding a far-reaching reversal of the 'European Method', the idea that significant areas of national life should be decided by laws proposed by the European Commission and settled between the European Parliament and a qualified majority of national ministers in the European Council. Britain complained – rightly – that the four freedoms were not even universally applied, with the Single Market in services remaining stubbornly incomplete despite numerous calls for progress in breaking down barriers such as mutual recognition of qualifications to match the harmonisation of standards that applied for goods. There was also a persistent feeling that the UK was more assiduous in applying all those European rules and regulations than some of the other member nations.

This book has assessed the areas where the EU impacts

most upon the UK. It has highlighted instances where the EU has been beneficial to communities in Britain, for example ensuring generous subsidies to reward farming and support regional development through good economic times and bad. It has also highlighted huge bureaucratic costs for business and industry such as the Working Time and Reach (chemicals) directives that would not have been devised by MPs in Westminster but were unavoidable due to EU membership. No system of governance is perfect and no one will agree with every law passed, which is why, at the national level, political parties are regularly voted in and out as the pendulum of public opinion swings for or against a particular choice of administration. One of the fundamental complaints about the EU, however, is that its form of democracy does not work like that. There is no pendulum. Whichever political movement is in the ascendant in the European Parliament, whoever is appointed to the role of European Commissioner and whichever national governments are represented in the European Council, the EU bandwagon seems to roll on in broadly the same direction of greater integration. As Günter Verheugen, the German member of the European Commission from 1999 to 2009, observed (before Croatia brought the membership total to twenty-eight nations):

There are twenty-seven commissioners, which means twenty-seven directorate-generals. And twenty-seven directorate-generals means that everyone needs to prove that they are needed by constantly producing new

directives, strategies or projects. In any case, the rule is:
More and more, more and more, all the time.

The higher-than-ever level of eurosceptic support
across the EU, and David Cameron's pledge to renegotiate Britain's relationship to show that powers can be
clawed back to national level, present a moment for
the European Union to show that it is responsive to
member state concerns. The challenge for the new
European Parliament, elected in May 2014, and the
new European Commission, appointed at the end of
2014, will be to adapt the EU for a new era. It would
be a huge mistake to ignore demands for a more flexible system. To do so would be to push the UK further
towards the exit, whichever party claims victory at the
2015 general election. If Labour wins without guaranteeing a referendum, it will be faced at some point with
a public vote under the EU Act 2011 when a significant
EU treaty change comes along – a vote that will be
hard to win, with defeat likely to trigger a wider ballot
on membership. Given the strength of feeling among
Conservatives, the party will enact Cameron's referendum promise whenever it returns to power.

How to vote, then, when the referendum comes? This
book has shown that in many of the key themes and
sectors affected by EU membership, there are strong
arguments on both sides of the fence. The weight of argument on Britain's place in the world is that it would be
diminished by leaving, an inevitable effect of detachment
from a regional power, and perhaps the unavoidable

fate anyway of a cash-strapped medium-sized country in the process of downsizing its armed forces and global diplomatic presence. If Britain was to leave the EU, inward investment may well fall, putting thousands of jobs at risk and threatening national income. But the negative impact in these areas will be negligible if Britain remains in the Single Market like Norway, or agrees a comprehensive Free Trade Agreement upon departure to retain open trading links. Unfortunately for voters, the precise nature of Britain's post-EU relationship will not be clear at the point of voting, adding another layer of uncertainty to an already complicated choice. If there were to be no penalties for leaving, other net contributor countries such as Sweden and Denmark could also be tempted to flee, meaning that Brussels will make sure that there are consequences for the first nation to call it a day. For an indication of how this might play out, keep an eye on Switzerland, which has three years to renegotiate its relationship following the vote to reject free movement for EU workers in February 2014.

Some of the benefits to be gained from leaving the EU that seemed obvious just a few years ago are a little less clear-cut today. The Common Fisheries Policy has long been a by-word for atrocious EU governance but has finally undergone reforms that seem to promise better management, closer to regional needs and more responsive to scientific advice. It is one area to watch closely to see if the new system works. On international trade, the European Commission failed for years to press forward with far-reaching Free Trade Agreements but seems at long last to have woken up to the world beyond its border region. The TTIP deal being negotiated with the US could finally demonstrate that there are substantial benefits from trusting the EU with the responsibility for international trade policy. If it delivers the economic gains claimed by its supporters, it could be a game-changer in the British debate about EU membership. It should be clear by the end of 2014 whether it will work. Closer to home, the EU rushed into green targets and mechanisms to combat climate change that have so far proved costly failures, such as the Emissions Trading System. There are some signs that a more realistic balance is being struck, including the decision to leave fracking to national governments and to back off from charging all airlines for emissions for the whole of any flight into the EU. Again only time, and the attitude of the new European Commission, will tell if Brussels can find the right blend of climate- and business-friendly green policies.

What, then, would be the positive advantages of leaving? Primarily it would mean opting out of the European political project, so that all legislative decisions and judicial oversight will once again be based on the British Isles – provided that membership of the Single Market through the European Economic Area is also rejected. Once again, this is unknowable at the point of casting a referendum ballot. If the UK left the EU only to join the EEA, then legislative decisions over farming, fishing, justice, policing, international trade policy, regional funding, transport, VAT and customs will return to these shores and become subject to UK courts, while employment and social regulations, the four freedoms, state aid, competition and consumer affairs policy, and most environmental regulation would stay under the EU and the European Court of Justice. As they mark their referendum ballot paper to stay or leave, voters are unlikely to know what the UK's post-EU status will be. It means in practice that only those comfortable with being outside the EU and the EEA should vote for Brexit, in line with UKIP policy for a Free Trade Agreement with Brussels and nothing more.

A complete break of this kind, in line with the UKIP position, means that Britain will be at liberty to reverse any EU rule or regulation accepted into domestic law. Many will not be removed because they protect air, food or water quality, or guarantee equal treatment for men and women in the workplace. An independent UK government will be free to introduce more 'flexibilities' for employers, such as scrapping the EU's minimum four-week paid annual holiday entitlement or abandoning the equal rights for agency workers after twelve weeks in a job. Other expensive requirements, such as holding open a post for a pregnant worker who leaves to have a baby, could be revoked for small and medium-sized businesses altogether. With the rest of the country freed from EU standards, the onus will be on exporters to ensure that they keep up to date with the latest technical and legal requirements agreed in Brussels if they want to trade with the continent. Whole areas of national life will return to domestic control, from regional funding to agricultural support to environmental protection and international trade policy – although any decision to cut tariffs to allow cheaper imports of food and other goods must be applied evenly to all markets under World Trade Organization rules. That will limit the ability to respond in kind to protectionist moves by Brussels following Brexit. VAT could be scrapped and replaced with a local sales tax to stimulate regional economies.

This book found that the sector most strongly against leaving the EU is the City of London. Under the 'complete break' scenario, thousands of jobs and billions of pounds in taxes could flee the country. The implications could be far-reaching – a drop in government income would need to be made up elsewhere, the withdrawal of significant support from wealthy bankers for the London property market could mean a house-price crash, and the long-term reduction in critical mass for the financial services industry could lead to a rebalancing of the British economy. For some, this provides ample reason for voting to leave the EU, while for others it will be a reason to stay. The picture could yet be complicated by more negative developments for the City from Brussels – and Frankfurt. If the European Central Bank has its way and starts grabbing euro-denominated business away from London, the balance in favour of staying in the EU could shift dramatically. Again, it is a case of watch this space.

In the end, the choice facing Britain boils down to the same clash of fundamental forces that underpinned the Swiss referendum result on EU migrants. On the one hand there is the defence of national identity and sovereignty which seeks to draw a line on openness to the world, while on the other hand there is the belief that only joint governance will ensure economic prosperity in full partnership with Britain's neighbours. Many of those who passionately want to leave the EU subscribe to those analysts who foresee no financial damage to the national balance sheet, or indeed economic benefits from Brexit, while Nigel Farage has said that he would 'rather we weren't slightly richer' if Britain could regain full border controls. Many of those who passionately want the UK to play a full part in the EU see no other way to deal with globalisation than sharing sovereignty to build a mighty European bloc. Most British voters lie somewhere between these two positions, torn between the ideal of open European cooperation and pulling up the drawbridge, with a feeling that in practice the EU experiment has gone too far. As David Cameron put it in his Bloomberg speech, 'democratic consent for the EU in Britain is now wafer thin'.

Opinion polls throughout 2013 suggested that without a meaningful renegotiation handing some powers back to the UK, the referendum is much more likely to result in Britain leaving. That gives the EU a chance to play a proactive role in persuading the British to stick with it. It could draw up plans to focus regional funding on the poorer member states and overhaul its out-dated system of farm subsidies, both of which would save billions of pounds and demonstrate a willingness to roll back central controls. Another powerful sign of modernisation would be to end the European Parliament's travelling circus by scrapping its monthly trek to Strasbourg. The EU still has a few more years before a likely UK referendum to prove its economic competence and convince British voters that it is fit for purpose in the twenty-first century – not only must it forge ahead with bilateral trade deals, it must also demonstrate its ability to solve the euro crisis and get southern Europe back to work.

The EU needs to provide clear safeguards to show that a member state can have a long-term future in the club without joining the single currency. That means stronger rights for non-euro countries to opt out of legislation, to demonstrate that the organisation has the flexibility to include Britain in the decades ahead. The EU could frame this reform as a new type of associate membership for those countries that reject the euro, keeping them in the Single Market while relaxing the requirement to take part in other aspects of integration, especially in the economic field but also in justice and social legislation. Senior figures in Brussels insist that there is no plan to create a United States of Europe. A new deal for the UK would prove it, and appeal to floating voters on Britain's EU membership who feel concerned that a decision to stay will mean the continual erosion of national sovereignty. It would establish the principle that membership is responsive to national traditions and that 'ever closer union' is a choice not a compulsion.

The likelihood of significant concessions to create a made-to-measure membership addressing every British concern is slim, however, especially given the competing demands of the other twenty-seven member states and the requirement for unanimous agreement. Britain is already the least integrated of the EU nations, outside of the euro and the Schengen passport-free travel zone, and a reluctant participant in further centralising measures. That is why the best thing that the EU can do between now and the British referendum is to press on with reforms to show that the new fishing policy or the ambitious trade deals are not exceptions but signs of things to come. Without the prospect of a better EU, there is no answer to the attractions of Brexit. Returning to sovereign control over domestic affairs and full responsibility for its destiny on the world stage, Britain will survive outside the EU despite the upheaval of leaving. The question is whether it will thrive. Paradoxically, one of the conditions for a successful divorce is the goodwill of the other partner. This book has highlighted the wide range of shared interests between the European nations and shown that some measure of compromise is inevitable. No perfect formula exists for the complete jigsaw of continental cooperation and Britain has much to lose from an acrimonious breakdown in relations with the European Union, in or out.

BRITAIN'S EU CONTRIBUTIONS, REBATE AND RECEIPTS

Year	Gross total	Rebate	Gross contribution	Public sector receipts	Net contribution
1973	181	n/a	181	79	102
1974	181	n/a	181	150	31
1975	342	n/a	342	398	56
1976	463	n/a	463	296	167
1977	737	n/a	737	368	369
1978	1,348	n/a	1,348	526	822
1979	1,606	n/a	1,606	659	947
1980	1,767	98	1,669	963	706
1981	2,174	693	1,481	1,084	397
1982	2,863	1,019	1,844	1,238	606
1983	2,976	807	2,169	1,522	647
1984	3,204	528	2,676	2,020	656
1985	3,940	227	3,713	1,905	1,808
1986	4,493	1,701	2,792	2,220	572
1987	5,202	1,153	4,049	2,328	1,721
1988	5,138	1,594	3,544	2,182	1,362
1989	5,585	1,154	4,431	2,116	2,315
1990	6,355	1,697	4,658	2,183	2,475
1991	5,807	2,497	3,309	2,765	544
1992	6,738	1,881	4,857	2,827	2,030
1993	7,985	2,539	5,446	3,291	2,155
1994	7,189	1,726	5,463	3,253	2,211

1995	8,889	1,207	**7,682**	3,665	**4,017**
1996	9,133	2,412	**6,721**	4,373	**2,348**
1997	7,991	1,733	**6,258**	4,661	**1,597**
1998	10,090	1,378	**8,712**	4,115	**4,597**
1999	10,287	3,171	**7,117**	3,479	**3,638**
2000	10,517	2,085	**8,433**	4,241	**4,192**
2001	9,379	4,560	**4,819**	3,430	**1,389**
2002	9,439	3,099	**6,340**	3,201	**3,139**
2003	10,966	3,559	**7,407**	3,728	**3,679**
2004	10,895	3,593	**7,302**	4,294	**3,008**
2005	12,567	3,656	**8,911**	5,329	**3,581**
2006	12,426	3,569	**8,857**	4,948	**3,909**
2007	12,456	3,523	**8,933**	4,332	**4,601**
2008	12,653	4,862	**7,791**	4,497	**3,294**
2009	14,129	5,392	**8,737**	4,401	**4,336**
2010	15,197	3,047	**12,150**	4,768	**7,382**
2011	15,357	3,143	**12,214**	4,132	**8,082**
2012	15,746	3,110	**12,636**	4,168	**8,468**
2013	17,184	3,324	**13,860**	5,237	**8,624**
TOTAL	**301,576**	**79,736**	**221,840**	**115,373**	**106,467**

Notes: All figures in £ million. Figures for 2013 are provisional; rebate column includes ad hoc refunds from 1980 until 1984 and some of the 1985 total when the rebate officially started (total of pure rebate is £76,530 million). Net contribution figure £1 million out in some years due to rounding.

Sources: 'The EU Budget', House of Commons Library Standard Note SN/EP/864; 'European Union Finances 2013', HM Treasury CM 8740.

NOTES

All figures correct at time of printing but subject to change as budgets are revised or updated. Historic budget figures given in prices of the day. Quotations taken from a range of authoritative sources including media reports, speeches and books listed in the bibliography; sources for figures included below.

1   European Court of Auditors Annual Report 2012, 5 November 2013
    http://www.eca.europa.eu/Lists/ECADocuments/PRAR12/a13_
    36.EN.pdf
2   'Van Rompuy's Egg to Cost 327 million', *Flanders News.be*, 3 May
    2013
    http://www.deredactie.be/cm/vrtnieuws.english/Brussels/
    1300503_Egg_Van_Rompuy
    'Skyrocketing Costs for Skyscraper Project', *Spiegel Online
    International*, 28 October 2013
    http://www.spiegel.de/international/business/cost-overruns-and-
    delays-plague-ecb-skyscraper-project-in-frankfurt-a-930352.html
3   Standard Eurobarometer 80, Autumn 2013
    http://ec.europa.eu/public_opinion/archives/eb/eb80/eb80_anx_
    en.pdf
4   Bojan Pancevski, '£1 billion for MEPs travelling circus', *Sunday
    Times*, 30 September 2012, p. 5.
5   The Price of a Multi-Seat European Parliament
    http://www.singleseat.eu/10.html
6   Bojan Pancevski, 'German Invasion Cuts Britons Out of Top
    Brussels Jobs', *Sunday Times*, 24 November 2013, p. 43.
7   *Time's Up! The case against the EU's 48-hour working week*,
    Open Europe, March 2009, p. 4.

8 'European Union, Trade in goods with Switzerland', Directorate General for Trade, 7 November 2013, p. 9
http://trade.ec.europa.eu/doclib/docs/2006/september/tradoc_113450.pdf

9 Camilla Cavendish, 'It's getting choppy but Britannia's 19 ships can't rule a single wave', *Sunday Times*, 22 September 2013, p. 29.

10 European Union External Action http://eeas.europa.eu/delegations/index_en.htm (Figures correct as of 22 February 2014) and European Union External Action http://eur-lex.europa.eu/budget/data/LBL2014/EN/SEC10.pdf

11 Office for National Statistics: Population by Country of Birth and Nationality Report, August 2013
http://www.ons.gov.uk/ons/rel/migration1/population-by-country-of-birth-and-nationality/2012/population-by-country-of-birth-and-nationality-report.html#tab-1--What-do-the-latest-figures-show-

12 Hansard, HL Deb, 4 February 2014, col. WA25-7.

13 'More than 3 in 4 want reduction in immigration', NatCen Social Research, 7 January 2014
http://www.natcen.ac.uk/news-media/press-releases/2014/january/more-than-3-in-4-want-reduction-in-immigration/

14 Brown, Scullion and Martin, 'Migrant Roma in the United Kingdom', October 2013
http://www.salford.ac.uk/environment-life-sciences/about/environment-and-life-sciences-news/study-finds-uk-has-200,000-roma-migrants

15 Ernst & Young's Attractiveness Survey UK 2013, pp. 4–5
http://www.ey.com/Publication/vwLUAssets/Ernst-and-Youngs-attractiveness-survey-UK-2013-No-room-for-complacency/$FILE/EY_UK_Attractiveness_2013.pdf

16 'World Investment Report 2013', United Nations Conference on Trade and Development
http://unctad.org/en/PublicationsLibrary/wir2013_en.pdf

17 UK Trade & Investment: Inward Investment Report 2012-13, p. 1
http://www.ukti.gov.uk/investintheuk/investintheukhome/item/553980.html

18 'Car manufacturing tops one million units for 2013', The Society of Motor Manufacturers and Traders, Press Release, 24 October 2013
http://www.smmt.co.uk/2013/10/car-manufacturing-tops-one-million-units-2013/

19 Office for National Statistics: Publication Tables UK Trade December 2013, 7 February 2014
http://www.ons.gov.uk/ons/taxonomy/index.html?nscl=Balance+of+Payments#tab-data-tables

20 Office for National Statistics: International Trade in Services 2012, 30 January 2014

http://www.ons.gov.uk/ons/dcp171778_351160.pdf
21 Hugo van Randwyck, EFTA or the EU (London, The Bruges Group, 2011), p. 21
   http://www.brugesgroup.com/EFTAorTheEU.pdf
22 Joana Taborda, 'Euro Area Unemployment Rate at 12% in December', Trading Economics, 31 January 2013
   http://www.tradingeconomics.com/euro-area/unemployment-rate
23 'European Union Finances 2013', HM Treasury, CM 8740, November 2013.
24 Christopher Howarth, Anna Kullmann and Pawel Swidlicki, More for Less: Making the EU's Farm policy Work for Growth and the Environment, Open Europe, p. 17
   http://www.openeurope.org.uk/Content/Documents/Pdfs/CAP_2012.pdf
25 'Allocation of EU structural funding across the UK', Department for Business, Innovation and Skills press release, 26 March 2013.
26 The European Economic Area and Norway Grants
   http://eeagrants.org/Who-we-are/Our-history
27 'The Swiss Contribution in brief', Federal Apartment Foreign Affairs
   http://www.contribution-enlargement.admin.ch/en/Home/The_Swiss_contribution
28 Vaughne Miller, 'How much legislation comes from Europe?', House of Commons Library Research Paper, 13 October 2010.
29 Hansard, HL Deb, 9 January 2006, col. WA10–11.
30 Will Dahlgreen, 'EU referendum: the red lines for swing voters', YouGov, 18 December 2013
   http://yougov.co.uk/news/2013/12/18/eu-referendum-red-lines-swing-voters/
31 Office for National Statistics: United Kingdom Economic Accounts Q4 2012, 27 March 2013, Table B6.
32 Ibid. Table B6B.
33 Office for National Statistics: Publication Tables UK Trade December 2013, 7 February 2014
   http://www.ons.gov.uk/ons/taxonomy/index.html?nscl=Balance+of+Payments#tab-data-tables
34 Henry Overman and Alan Winters, 'North and South', CentrePiece, Winter 2004.
35 'Note considering the impact of EU membership on trade and consequent welfare effects', UK Trade and Investment
   https://www.gov.uk/government/uploads/system/uploads/attachment_data/file/220968/foi_eumembership_trade.pdf
36 'World Trade Developments 2010', World Trade Organization, 2011.
37 'International Trade Statistics 2011', World Trade Organization, 2011

http://www.wto.org/english/res_e/statis_e/its2011_e/its11_world_trade_dev_e.pdf

38 'Report highlights UK export growth in Korea', UK Trade and Investment South Korea, 4 October 2013
https://www.gov.uk/government/world-location-news/report-highlights-uk-exports-growth-in-korea

39 'World population to 2300', United Nations Department of Economic and Social Affairs, 2004
https://www.un.org/esa/population/publications/longrange2/WorldPop2300final.pdf

40 'World Trade Developments', World Trade Organization, 2011
http://www.wto.org/english/res_e/statis_e/its2011_e/its11_world_trade_dev_e.pdf

41 'Estimating the economic impact on the UK of a TTIP agreement between the EU and the US', Centre for Economic Policy Research, March 2013, pp. 32–3.

42 'Budget Report 2012 to 2014', Court of Justice of the European Union
http://eur-lex.europa.eu/budget/data/DB2014/EN/SEC04.pdf

43 'Key facts about UK financial and professional services', TheCityUK, 16 January 2014
https://www.thecityuk.com/research/our-work/reports-list/key-facts-about-uk-financial-and-related-professional-services/

44 ComRes: http://www.comres.co.uk/polls/Open_Europe_Final_tables_14th_December11.pdf

45 Figures provided by the European Commission directorate for Research, Innovation and Science for this book.

46 'Students in Higher Education Institutions 2011-12', Higher Education Statistics Agency.

47 '2012 UK Greenhouse Gas Emissions Final Figures', National Statistics, 4 February 2014, p. 4.

48 'Top 100 Regulations', Open Europe Briefing Note, 21 October 2013
http://www.openeurope.org.uk/Page/SingleMarket/en/live

49 'European Union Finances 2013', HM Treasury, CM 8740, November 2013.

50 Jason Cowley, 'How we pay for our richest landowners', The New Statesman, 19 September 2012
http://www.newstatesman.com/politics/politics/2012/09/how-we-pay-our-richest-landowners

51 'Farm business Income by type of farm in England 2012-13', Department for Environment, Food & Rural Affairs press release, 31 October 2013.

52 'CFP reform – Transferable Fishing Concessions'
ec.europa.eu/fisheries/reform/docs/tfc_en.pdf

53 'Statistics on UK Official Development Assistance', Department
   for International Development, 21 October 2013.
54 Juan Carlos Concepcion, 'Top 10 recipients of EU aid', Devex,
   9 September 2013
   https://www.devex.com/en/news/top-10-recipients-of-eu-aid/81760
55 'Annual report 2013 on the EU's Development and External
   Assistance policies and their implementation in 2012', European
   Commission, December 2013.
56 'Air passenger transport in the EU27', Eurostat news release
   161/2013, 5 November 2013.
57 Eurotunnel 2012 Annual Results, 21 March 2013.
58 easyJet Annual Report and Accounts 2013, 18 November 2013.

BIBLIOGRAPHY

Bache, Ian and George, Stephen, *Politics in the European Union* (Oxford: Oxford University Press, 2006)

Bennett, Chappell, Reed and Sriskandarajah, *Trading Places: The Commonwealth Effect Revisited* (London: Royal Commonwealth Society, 2010)

Booth, Howarth, Persson and Scarpetta, *Continental Shift: Safeguarding the UK's Financial Trade in a Changing Europe* (London: Open Europe, 2011)

Booth, Howarth, Scarpetta, *Tread Carefully: The Impact and Management of EU Free Movement and Immigration Policy* (London: Open Europe, 2012)

Campbell Bannerman, David, *The Ultimate Plan B: A Positive Vision of an Independent Britain outside the European Union* (Cambridge: David Campbell Bannerman, 2011)

Charter, David, *Au Revoir, Europe: What if Britain left the EU?* (London: Biteback Publishing, 2012)

Crafts, Nicholas, *Fifty Years of Economic Growth in Western Europe* (London: World Economics, 2004)

Drew, John and Bond, Martyn (editors), *The UK & Europe: Costs, Benefits, Options. The Regent's Report 2013* (London: Regent's University, 2013)

Duff, Andrew, *On Governing Europe* (London: Policy Network and ALDE, 2012)

Eichengreen, Barry and Boltho, Angela, *The Economic Impact of European Integration* (London: Centre for Economic Policy Research, 2008)

Ernst & Young, *Attractiveness Survey UK 2013: No Room for Complacency* (London: EYGM Ltd, 2013)

Fram, Nicholas, *Decolonization, the Commonwealth, and British Trade 1945–2004* (Stanford: Stanford University, 2006)

Fresh Start Project, *Options for Change Green Paper: Renegotiating the UK's Relationship with the EU* (London: 2012)

Fresh Start Project, *Manifesto for Change: A New Vision for the UK in Europe* (London: 2013)

Fresh Start Project, *Mandate for Reform: Securing the Right Deal for the UK* (London: 2013)

Gaskell, Sarah and Persson, Mats, *Still Out of Control* (London: Open Europe, 2010)

Heath, Edward, *Travels: People and Places in My Life* (London: Sidgwick & Jackson, 1977)

Hennessy, Peter, *The Prime Minister: The Office and Its Holders Since 1945* (London: Penguin Books, 2001)

Hindley, Brian and Howe, Martin, *Better Off Out?* (London: The Institute of Economic Affairs, 2001)

Howarth, Kullman and Swidlicki, *More for Less: Making the EU's Farm Policy Work for Growth and the Environment* (London: Open Europe, 2012)

Ilzkovitz, Dierx, Kovacs and Sousa, *Steps Towards a Deeper Economic Integration: The Internal Market in the 21st Century* (European Economics Papers 271, 2007).

Kellner, Peter, *Worried Nationalists, Pragmatic Nationalists and Progressive Internationalists – Who Might Win a British Referendum on Europe?* (London: European Council on Foreign Relations, 2012)

Leach, Graeme, *EU Membership, What's the Bottom Line?* (London: Institute of Directors, 2000)

Milne, Ian, *A Cost Too Far?* (London: Civitas, The Institute for the Study of Civil Society, 2004)

Milne, Ian and Hamill, Natalie, *Withdrawal from the EU Would Not Damage our Car Industry: True or False?* (London: Civitas, The Institute for the Study of Civil Society, 2012)

Monti, Mario, *A New Strategy for the Single Market* (Brussels: European Commission, 2010)

Open Europe, *The Rise of the EU Quangos* (London: Open Europe, 2012)

Persson, Gaskell and Booth, *Time's Up! The Case Against the EU's 48-hour Working Week* (London: Open Europe, 2009)

Piris, Jean-Claude, *The Future of Europe* (Cambridge, Cambridge University Press, 2012)

Rentoul, John, *Tony Blair: Prime Minister* (Little, Brown and Company, 2001)

Reynolds, David, *The Origins of the Cold War in Europe: International Perspectives* (New Haven, Yale University Press, 1994)

Seldon, Anthony with Peter Snowdon and Daniel

Collings, *Blair Unbound* (London: Simon & Schuster, 2007)

Straathof, Linders, Lejour and Moehlmann, *The Internal Market and the Dutch Economy*, (The Hague: Netherlands Bureau for Economic Policy Analysis, 2008)

Swidlicki, Ruparel, Persson and Howarth, *Off target: The Case for Bringing Regional Policy Back Home* (London: Open Europe, 2012)

Wall, Stephen, *A Stranger in Europe* (Oxford: Oxford University Press, 2008)

Winters, L. Alan, *Britain in Europe, A Survey of Quantitative Trade Studies*, (London: Centre for Economic Policy Research, 1986)

Young, Hugo, *This Blessed Plot: Britain and Europe from Churchill to Blair* (London: Papermac, 1999)

Broadcasts

European Funding, *File on 4*, BBC Radio 4, 17 July 2012

The EU Debate, *File on 4*, BBC Radio 4, 8 August 2012

Speech

Cameron, David, EU speech at Bloomberg, 23 January 2013 (online at https://www.gov.uk/government/speeches/eu-speech-at-bloomberg)

GLOSSARY

Common Agricultural Policy (CAP): The European Union's system of subsidies for farmers.

Council of the European Union: Forum for national ministers to meet and take policy and legislative decisions.

Economic and Monetary Union (EMU): The system underpinning the single currency.

Euro: The European single currency shared by eighteen nations.

European Central Bank: Administers monetary policy for the countries in the single currency, based in Frankfurt.

European Commission: Executive body of the European Union responsible for administration, oversight and proposing legislation.

European Commissioner: Member of the European Commission cabinet (known as the college, comprising one representative from all twenty-eight EU member states).

European Council: EU institution where leaders from the member states meet to set policy.

European Court of Human Rights (ECHR): Court in

Strasbourg that upholds the European Convention on Human Rights. It is not part of the European Union.

European Court of Justice (ECJ): Court based in Luxembourg that upholds and interprets EU law, comprised of one judge from each member state.

European Economic Area (EEA): Thirty-one countries (EU plus Iceland, Liechtenstein and Norway) that take part in the Single Market and adopt all relevant EU laws.

European Economic Community (EEC): Forerunner of the EU, which changed under the Maastricht Treaty of 1993.

European External Action Service: Diplomatic corps and overseas representation of the EU.

European Free Trade Association (EFTA): Four-country group (Iceland, Liechtenstein, Norway and Switzerland) originally set up with more countries including the UK in 1960 as an alternative to the EEC.

European Parliament: Elected body of the EU for revising laws comprised of 751 Members of the European Parliament (MEPs) including seventy-three from the UK.

European Union (EU): Economic and political alliance of twenty-eight nations synonymous with its main location in Brussels and built upon a series of treaties starting with the Treaty of Rome in 1957.

Four freedoms: The basis of the Single Market: the free movement of capital, goods, people and services.

Qualified Majority Voting (QMV): Method of deciding matters between ministers in the Council of the EU that attaches extra weight to bigger countries in a complicated formula.

Schengen: Name taken from a border town in Luxembourg for the European visa-free travel zone joined by twenty-six countries.

Single Market: EU customs-free internal trading area established by the Single European Act of 1986 with a Common External Tariff for imports.

Structural funds: EU aid for infrastructure projects in poorer areas.

Subsidiarity: Principle enshrined in the Maastricht Treaty that the EU shall only act when the objectives cannot be better met at national level.

ACKNOWLEDGEMENTS

I would like to thank Iain Dale and the whole team at Biteback Publishing for their belief and enthusiasm, particularly James Stephens for his encouragement and Hollie Teague for her wise editing. I am grateful to John Witherow, editor of *The Times*, and Richard Beeston, our much-missed foreign editor, for providing me with the opportunity to experience the European Union at first hand as a foreign correspondent for a great newspaper. I also have a huge debt of gratitude to my immediate colleagues in *The Times* foreign news department for comradeship and support.

There are many other people to thank for their kind assistance with this book, including: Dennis Abbott, Tim Aker, Eva Baumann, Anthony Browne, David Campbell Bannerman, Stephen Cave, John Clancy, Richard Corbett, Neil Corlett, Chris Cummings, Barry Deas, Andrew Duff, Nigel Farage, Patrizio Fiorilli, Richard Freedman, Antony Gravili, Mark Gray, Martin Haworth, Joe Hennon, James Holtum, Chantal Hughes, Michael Jennings, Syed Kamall, Sony Kapoor, Helen Kearns, Maja Kocijancic, Denis MacShane, Edward McMillan-Scott, Ian Milne, David Poyser, Fredrik

Sejersted, Struan Stevenson, Ulf Sverdrup, Jonathan Todd, Gawain Towler, Marjory Van Den Broeke, Roger Waite, Jon Worth and those who talked to me off the record, as well as my former Brussels colleagues Stephen Castle, Jacki Davis, Geoff Meade, Bojan Pancevski, Nicci Smith, Ian Traynor, Bruno Waterfield and Rory Watson for the many conversations over the years. All mistakes, omissions and misunderstandings are mine. Last, but not least, I am eternally grateful to my parents, Leonard, Sheila, Liz, Ray and Mikey for their support and especially to Michelle and Leo without whom none of this makes any sense at all.

Berlin, February 2014

Also available from Biteback Publishing

THE BATTLE FOR BRITAIN
David Torrance

On 18 September 2014, Scots will decide their future: should the country quit the United Kingdom and take control of its own destiny, or should it remain part of what advocates call the most successful political and economic union of modern times?

With access to the strategists and opinion-makers on both sides of the political divide, this book goes straight to the heart of the great debate, providing an incisive, authoritative, occasionally trenchant guide to the most dramatic constitutional question of our times – the battle for Britain.

384pp paperback, £14.99
Available from all good bookshops or order from
www.bitebackpublishing.com

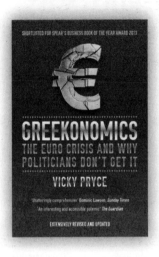